Commander Crystal Steiner, The Prodigal Daughter

Book Two

Robert D. Jensen

Contents

Dedication

To my readers.

To every father and daughter who has lost each other.

Acknowledgments

I want to thank my editor, Robert Cahill. With his help, this book was completed. Thank you for your patience, guidance, and use of the editor's red pen.

About the Author

Robert Jensen is a retired Millwright living in British Columbia, Canada. His lifelong dream to become a writer began with a biography of his wife, Eileen's grandmother, who emigrated to Canada from Europe in 1909. After completing this family book, Robert decided to write his first book, "Captain Styler Is My Name," which was first published in 2017. His second book, Commander Crystal Steiner Is My Name," was published in 2018 for the first time.

You may contact Robert at bookofexcelllence@aol.com

Lists of Characters

Sector One

Solar System – 'Academy'

Planet – Academy

New Commonwealth Navy Search and Rescue

- ***Commander Crystal A. Styler Steiner:***

Pilot, Captain Tom's wife & Captain Mark Styler's daughter

- ***Captain Tom Steiner***

Assistant Administrator for the Navy Search and Rescue, Former Private Contractor Cryptologic Technician for the

Commonwealth Navy Security

- ***Captain Mark Styler***

Owner/Operator of the ship *Marvel* and a Merchant Trader

- ***Katherine (Katy) Stevenson Styler***

Crystal's mother, former princess, Owner/Operator of the ship *Marvel* and a Merchant Trader

Commodore Derek Massey

Administrator for the Navy Search and Rescue

- ***Sharon Giezer (Grace Morrison)***

Tom's former girlfriend, former Spy Agent, and later a Warden

- ***Sheba Steiner***

Tom's mother, Journalist for the local media. A former Journalist for the Navy Security

- ***Andy Liu***

Parts clerk, Tom's close friend and hacker.

- ***Allen Bergen***

Tom's former student, a Navy recruiter, and later a Captain

Commissioner "Breeze" of the Navy Search and Rescue

- ***Commander Crystal A. Steiner***

Commanded the ship *Breeze*

- ***Doctor Shan McGee***

Civilian, Private Doctor, and Neurologist

- ***Sergeant Miller***

Marine Intelligence Agent

- ***Lieutenant Giannis***

Pilot

- ***Rear Admiral T. A. Melnyk***

Tom's father

- ***Commodore Doctor Halley***

Neurologist, Memory Specialist

Sector Three, Solar System Sunna, Planet New Sweoland, King Stevenson's Palace:

- ***Crystal Styler***

Captain Mark and Katherine's daughter, the King's granddaughter

- ***Jayson Stevenson***

King Stevenson's son, Prince and Crystal's uncle

Jennifer Stevenson

Jayson's wife

- ***Jenny Stevenson***

Jayson's daughter

- ***'King' Stevenson***

Jayson's father, Crystal's grandfather

- ***Terry***

Palace Inspector

- **Mr. Jonesborough**

Relief Palace Inspector

- **Doctor Shan McGee**

Family Doctor, and Jayson's friend

Shelia McGee (Doctor Shan's daughter)

- **Sheba Webber**

Investigative Journalist, Tom's mother

- **Captain Ted Fredrickson**

Captain of the King Stevenson's Yacht, *'The Nyfodte'*

- **Tanya**

Bert's wife and Jayson's niece

- **Midway**

a dwarf planet, a solid iron 3034-mile-wide asteroid, located between Sector Two and the territory of Sector Five

- **Samantha Stevenson**

Crystal's great grandmother, director of Midway

- **Tom Beegle**

(Tom Steiner)

- **Shelia McGee**

(Crystal)

- ***Bert***

Illegal person, a genetic offspring

- ***Android***

Synthetic organic entities with limited emotional aspects to their personalities. Androids were created as alternatives to the robots. All androids in the Commonwealth work under strict regulations and most androids provide more than just manual labor, depending on how they are programmed. Similar in height as humans, greyish skinned with white blood.

- ***Penitentiary Colony***

Located in Sector Two, near the territory Sector Five

Alliance solar system – Planet Green Shield, located in the territory Sector Five

- ***Tony***

Surveyor team leader, a small private contractor for the Commonwealth

- ***Jon***

Biologist employee

- ***Genet***

Biologist employee

- *Karl*

Surveyor and geologist employee

- ***Planet Green Shield Natives***

Rexes and the Grunts

- ***Anirudh***

Rexes' Hunting leader

- ***Diya***

Rexes' second leader

- ***Grunts Elder***

Tiff

- ***Thracian Empire***

When first discovered, little was known of the Thracian Empire. The Old Earth ancient name "Thracian" was given because of their ferocious warlike society.

- ***Commander Casingat (Casey)***

A Langat Klan member, Thracian Renegade Leader, and later a diplomat

Lizard Planet – Located in Sector Two

- ***Howard Hanford***

Police

- **Gloria Hanford**

Tour Guide and Howard's wife, Tom's mother

- **Akia Contee**

Lawyer

- **Rebecca G. Hein**

Android impersonator, hired assassin

- **Captain Chloe**

Commonwealth Navy Security, Rebecca's daughter

- **Academy Navy Secret Court**

Navy Court Martial Hearing

- **Counsellor Stamkos**

Civilian

- **Inspector Jonesborough**

Civilian Inspector

- **Lea Lam**

Judge: Chairwoman

- **Major Paulina Craig**

Tom's lawyer

Time Frame

2367. Mark Styler and Katherine (Kate) Stevenson married on the planet 'New Sweoland'

2368. Crystal Styler is born on the ship *Marvel*

2385. Crystal at age 17 enters the university on the planet 'New Sweoland'

2386. Katherine dies

2390. Crystal's banishment

2390. Crystal meets Tom Steiner

2391. Commonwealth-Thracian War

2392. Stevenson home-world, civil war destruction

2392. Commonwealth-Thracian Empire War ends

2393. Crystal's memory is restored

2394. Crystal and Tom leave 'Midway'

2395. Crystal and Tom leave planet 'Green Shield'

2395. Crystal and Tom marry

2396. Crystal and Tom sign up for the 'Navy Search and Rescue'

2406. Crystal's Court Martial, (Hearing)

2417. Tom and Crystal's anniversary, Tom meets his mother

2426. Civil War and the reformation of the New Commonwealth

2427. Crystal commands the ship *Breeze* and locates the ship *Marvel*

Introduction

Crystal, a princess by birthright from New Sweoland, was raised by her mother and father on the ship '*Marvel*', a merchant trader ship. While Crystal was attending New Sweoland's university, she became a bitter, angry woman, as she blamed her father for the death of her beloved mother, Katherine. Unbeknownst to Crystal, the king had hidden the truth about her parents and the nearby danger. When the king died, Crystal was covertly exiled from New Sweoland. Afterward, Crystal learned that she had been manipulated and betrayed by people she loved, and her memory had been blocked. Would she love and trust ever again?

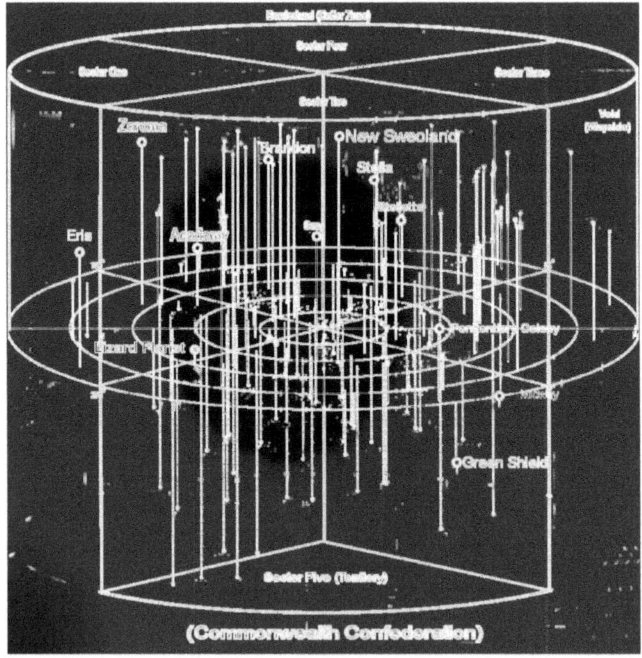

Chapter 1

I was an only and lonely child in a family-run merchant trader business, cruising among a vast four-sector star system called the 'Commonwealth'. My only friends were my parents, Mark and Katherine, the ship's computer, Sara, the ship's cook, Bill, and sometimes, the rotating crews aboard the *Marvel*. By the time I was 17 years old, I was a typical rebellious and obnoxious teenager. It was agreed that I would return to Planet New Sweoland, where my grandfather was a king, as my mother was a former princess, to further my education.

Many people I have known have told me that our characters are determined by how we are raised. My parents believe that God made me the way I am—if there is a God. Five years later, and four years after my mother died, an unexpected event took place that drastically changed my life course. Crystal Aileen Styler Steiner is my name, and this is my story.

The Present: Year 2427

Sector One

Solar System: Academy

Planet: Academy

New Commonwealth Navy Search and Rescue

Administration Briefing Room

Present: Commodore Dereck Massey and Captain Tom Steiner

"You look tired, Commodore."

"I am tired, and let's be less formal here, Tom. The Commonwealth Navy Security is going to be very unhappy with us! We would have lost our assignment if I hadn't had help from the top brass and elites. Besides, as Navy Search and Rescue, the assignment is legally ours! The Navy Security is also a hundred times bigger than us, so we must submit our assignment to them sooner or later. Tom, how soon can we get our new ship off-world?"

"Derek, our ship hasn't been fully tested yet, and I am hesitant to allow an untested ship to take this assignment."

"All the more reason I want this ship off-world. The Navy Security would be completely caught off guard. Tom, you know how important this assignment is for us."

"Derek, we may have to watch our backs once our ship is off-world. Even though there has been a huge shakeup in the Navy Security recently, I still don't trust them."

"I agree with you, Tom, but we still have friends upstairs when needed.

"What about our ship?"

Tom sighed, "All right, we've got a good crew on board. The enlisted members are mainly our standard test crew to cover our tracks. Because this assignment is unusual, I requested a civilian—Doctor Shan."

"I've heard of him. Can he be trusted?" Derek asked.

"I'd stake my reputation on it."

"Alright, who do we have to take on this assignment?"

With a firm voice, Tom replied, "Commander C.A. Steiner!"

Derek's eyes opened wide in alarm. "Tom, are you sure about this?"

"Derek, I don't like this any more than you do, but Commander Steiner is more qualified to take on this assignment. Besides, she has every right to take on this task!"

Derek leaned back in his chair, "I suppose you are right. Has Commander Steiner been briefed yet?"

"Not yet. Commander Steiner will be briefed in 30 minutes, and the ship will be off-world in one hour."

"That's what I want to hear. Carry on."

***

Tom stood alone inside the hanger facing the Navy Search and Rescue's newest ship, the fastest ever built. On the side of the ship, he could see the name *Breeze*. Tom heard the hangar door open and heard footsteps echo inside the building. Someone approached behind him.

"Commander Steiner, reporting for duty!"

Tom turned to face Crystal, a woman with the most beautiful smile. One he was accustomed to seeing and fortunate to be in love with and married to. She was tall and petite, with sandy blond hair. Even though she was 58 years of age, like most people, her age appearance had been stopped between 35 to 40 years. Modern medical science maintained individuals' youthful age until the unexplained threshold of 120, at which point the body would quickly break down within a year. Some people believed the Creator had set the age limit at 120.

"Good morning, Commander. Sorry for the rush and secrecy. Your crew will be here in five minutes, so we are alone for now."

Crystal dropped her formal tone and approached her husband comfortably, "Tom, what's going on? This is highly unusual and beyond protocol. Why did the New Commonwealth give us this ship?"

"It is indeed unusual but quite necessary," replied Tom. "As for why we have this ship, it is the result of the recent disaster on a commercial liner 30 light years away. Our ship was too slow to rescue the passengers and crew. Over forty VIPs among the passengers lost their lives. These VIPs represent ten political giants of the New Commonwealth. Despite the Navy Military Security's objection, we are the first to receive the newest hyperwarp drive. This ship can take on 150 passengers with only 15 crew members. She is fast; your destination is only 2.8 days at warp speed. The Commonwealth's fastest ship takes 7.8 days, so you will have a five-day head start on their fastest ship." Tom handed over the ship's electronic notepad to Crystal. "As for your assignment, you and your crew will be immediately notified of your assignment after the warp jump."

"Tom, why all the secrecy? We are only a search and rescue."

With a stern look, Tom replied, "We know where Mark is, and soon so will the Navy military security."

Suddenly, everything is so obvious! Crystal thought.

"Everything will be explained after the jump. According to the scheduled testing protocol, you have only 30 minutes to get this ship off-world." Tom added.

"Why me?" Crystal asked.

"Mark has plenty of good reasons not to trust anyone else, so choosing you makes perfect sense."

"Tom, I let him down a long time ago."

"We all have family squabbles, but most of us get over them. Don't we, Crystal?" Tom smiled. "Time is up. Get going and bring back your Mark."

"Yes, sir," Crystal stepped back and saluted.

Tom sighed. "Crystal," he said dryly.

"I can't," Crystal protested.

"You still have 30 seconds before your crew shows up!"

Crystal smiled, grabbed both of Tom's ears, and kissed him hard. "Captain!"

"Commander," Tom replied as she turned and boarded the ship. Tom turned to exit the hangar as the ship's crew began to come inside. "Your Commander is waiting for your men inside the ship," Tom said with a straight face. He gave a quick look back at the ship and said in a quiet voice, "Good luck, Crystal. Darn, my ears hurt!"

***

The pilot announced, "Commander, warp jump will begin in 5, 4, 3, 2, 1."

When the odd yet familiar feeling of the warp jump was soon past, Crystal asked for the roll call on the bridge. When the crew and the civilian Doctor Shan were on the bridge, Crystal studied the faces around her. All the crew was well-seasoned, experienced personnel. The Commander's request on the bridge confused the crew because they had never met her before.

When the last crew member showed up, Crystal said, "Ship Computer, ENGAGE CODE PROJECT MARVEL, 646280."

A holographic image appeared in the middle of the bridge—the computer generated an image of Commodore Derek, who spoke before them all.

"As you can see, I am a computerized image of Commodore Derek. Any questions you have may be asked after you are briefed. Your usual assignment has been altered and kept top secret from the highest administrators. All testing protocols have been suspended, and our destination has been rerouted to a star system 38.7 light years away. Our mission as New Commonwealth Search and Rescue is to find and bring home Captain Mark Styler, his crew, and, if possible, the ship *Marvel*."

Everyone was stunned to hear the news of the announcement about the legendary hero. "Before you ask any questions, I'll give you a brief history. One year ago, one of *Marvel*'s escape pods entered one of the main merchant shipping routes, and an open-line transmission from the pod was sent. Unfortunately, one of the Commonwealth Navy Security ships was stationed nearby and clamped down on the transmission. All the nearby merchant ships were raided, and the recorded messages were taken. When the merchant traders learned of the transmission from one of their own, political pressure mounted to force Navy Security to release the transmission to the public. The Navy Security modified the transmission before releasing it to the public."

"You all have been officially told that Captain Styler and his ship were attacked by two Thracian scout ships, raided, and killed before returning to their home world. Another part of the original transmission was smuggled and placed in the hands of a merchant guild member, Stacy Rand, in Sector Five at the New Wayside Station. The old Wayside merchant trader station, as you may remember, was located in the 'Void' in Sector One near the Thracian borderland, an area in which there are no stars or planetary objects within a ten-light-year distance from the nearest star system near the Borderline. The station was abandoned because of the Commonwealth/Thracian war threat, and their operation was moved to Sector Five."

"When Navy Security learned the whereabouts of the smuggled recorded message, the security forces raided Wayside Station. Unknown to Navy Security, their devices failed to shut down the Wayside cam and the new Warp Net communication. Stacy's assassination and the truth about Captain Styler were revealed in minutes among the Five Sectors through Warp Net."

"The original official records show that 37 years ago, the Navy Brass took full credit for destroying the Robots' secret home base. One year ago, when Captain Styler forwarded the news of the Robots and the Cyborgs, the whereabouts of their home-world base, and their plan to re-establish their original war against humanity 100 years ago, it made him a hero. That information was given to Navy Security more than 38 years ago. Lastly, the several failed assassinations attempt against Captain Styler and the murder of his two crew members were the tipping point for the general population. The Navy Security's need to cover up the knowledge of the surviving Robots' past rebellion at the expense of human lives was too much for the general public."

"The Five Sectors' administrators were fed up with the dictatorial power, the political elites, and the Navy Security's corruption. The civil war was underway among the Five Sectors. One year after the Civil War was over, the New Commonwealth was founded. The Navy Security headquarters had been heavily damaged, so a private contractor was hired to clean it up. Two days ago, the rest of the original transmission was discovered. We now know the location of Captain Styler and his android, Chantal, but so does the Navy Security, and although their agenda is unknown, they badly wanted the assignment."

"Since overhauling the Navy's structure, we no longer have to answer to the Navy Security, but to the New Commonwealth. If Captain Styler and his android are alive, we will bring them to the New Commonwealth Headquarters for their safety."

"Permission to speak, sir."

The computer image of Commodore Derek turned toward the speaker. "Go ahead, Sergeant Miller."

"Why is there a conflict with the Navy Security? I thought their house had been overhauled?"

"Thank you, Sergeant. It's true that their inner circle has been replaced, but because of their bloated bureaucracy, the New Commonwealth feels that some of the lower bureaucrats should be appointed because of their knowledge of Navy Security's systematic structure. There's still a risk of foul play within Navy Security toward Captain Styler."

"I have another question. With all due respect to Commander Steiner, where is Commander Matheson?" Miller asked.

"A good question, Sergeant. We believe he would resist any effort to cooperate with us. Therefore, we appointed Commander Steiner to assist us."

"What could Commander Steiner do that Commander Matheson could not?" Miller asked.

"I can answer that," said Crystal. "My maiden name is Styler."

"How are you related to Captain Mark Styler?" asked the Sergeant.

"Captain Mark Styler," Crystal paused for a second, then added, "is my father!"

***

The notepad's holographic images of Commodore Steiner's desk faded away. *A whole year wasted because of the elites' pathetic political decision-making*, Crystal thought. *And why does this have to happen? It still makes no sense? Since when does anything ever make sense?*

Crystal felt her temper increasing until the memory of Tom's voice took over. *Anger is not a tool!*

Crystal took a deep breath as her temper subsided. *I'd better be careful here. I can't afford to let my temper get in my way again. My uncontrolled anger caused far too many past mistakes.* Crystal thought, *The guilt of letting my father down is still on my mind.*

For the first time, Crystal looked around her quarters. The room was typical Navy and Rescue: a gun-metal hall with a minimum padded wall, with only a printed photo of a young family near the bed's headboard. Slight guilt took over when she realized it was Commodore McDonnell's family. *Twelve hours have gone by, and I am exhausted.*

"Room Computer, I wish not to be disturbed for one hour unless it is important," Crystal ordered.

"Acknowledged," replied the room computer.

Crystal lay down on the bed facing the ceiling. "Lights out," Crystal ordered. The room darkened, and she quickly fell asleep.

***

Chapter 2

The Reminiscence Year 2390, 37 years before the present.

Solar System Sunna, Planet: New Sweoland, Stevenson's Palace.

Feeling tired and light-headed, Crystal decided to walk back to her bedroom and bumped into the unopened door. She was shocked and hurt that the door ignored her, so she commanded her bedroom door to open. She stepped into her room and saw a man sitting on her chair.

"Uncle Jayson, what are you doing in my room? And how did you bypass the security?"

"Door," said Jayson in a quiet, tired voice, "Close and secure this room. Before you let your temper get the best of you, I suggest you sit down and hear what I say."

"Not very likely," said Crystal. "Door, open." The door did not respond. Crystal turned and said, "Uncle Jayson, Grandfather will not approve of this!"

"Your grandfather, or should I say, my father, is dead. To be more accurate, he was murdered."

Crystal's face turned white, and her eyes looked frightened as she sat on the chair. "Murdered? Who would want to do away with my grandfather?"

"Quite a few individuals. The problem is finding the right person or group. A conspiracy to murder the king has been going on for quite some time."

Crystal stood up angrily and said, "Then we need to arrest them all to get to the bottom of this. Get our chief of staff, Terry, on this now; he will know what to do. And while you're at it, I want you to lock down all the..."

"Crystal, you are the most arrogant, selfish, sarcastic, ill-tempered young princess."

"Uncle Jayson, I believe that you…"

"Your beliefs don't make you a better person; your behavior does. And your behavior is a dishonor to your father's and mother's names! You are truly a disgrace to Mark's name!"

"Uncle Jayson, you have no business talking to me like that and bringing up my father! He murdered my mother!" Crystal cried.

Jayson sighed, "I always doubted Mark murdering Katie."

"If Grandfather heard you say that, he would make an example of you," said Crystal.

"You are quite right, so I always kept my peace." Jayson rose from the chair and walked to the window. Father became paranoid in the last few years, and as king, he had become perplexed. Two hours ago, I entered Father's private den and found him dead, with one of his projectile handguns in his hand."

Crystal was speechless to learn of her grandfather's death.

"Many years ago, my father told me that if something were to happen to him, I would give the den room a computer code. For almost two hours, various documents were downloaded to my implant."

"What was in those documents?" Crystal asked.

Jayson replied, "There were different finance documents and information on political dealings and security breaches."

"What security breaches?" Crystal asked.

Jayson turned to face her, "Assassination attempts. There were three attempts to kill my father in the past, as well as two attempts on me and one on you."

"But why?" Crystal cried. "Grandfather was a good man and king! His people loved him!" Crystal shouted.

"As I said, not everyone," Jayson said dryly. "There are those who want a share of the power, not to mention that others wanted a Republican. I agree; he was a good man, but he had his faults."

Jayson placed a black memory disc on the table near her.

"What is on the disc?" Crystal asked.

"The truth about your father and mother. Crystal, your grandfather lied to you."

"Grandfather would never lie to me," Crystal cried.

"Unfortunately, he did. Be prepared to face the truth; it is not pretty. I will return in an hour; this room will be secured for your protection."

Jayson exited the room before Crystal could say anything, leaving her a prisoner. For a moment, Crystal was overwhelmed with mixed emotions; then, her anger rose up inside her. "Grandfather would never lie to me," she said as she picked up the disc and inserted it in the receiver. A 3D image appeared near her, showing four people in space suits running away from someone. *This video must be taken from the ship,* Marvel, Crystal thought.

She recognized her father's and mother's space suits among the four. *The other two must be Bill, the chef, and Timothy, the drive engineer*, she thought. They were firing back with their stunners at the unseen enemy. Crystal knew who they were: the Thracians—a mighty warrior society beyond the borderlands of the Commonwealth's four sectors.

A shot from a Thracian's stunner hit her father as he buckled to the ground.

A Thracian stepped aside from the boulder and aimed at her father with a G-gun, a universally feared weapon that causes the body's cells to separate from the bio-glue that holds them together. Then, Crystal witnessed what her grandfather had lied to her about. Her mother knew what was about to happen, and she ran to shield Mark from the dreadful effect of the G-gun. Her suit expanded and burst from the explosion of her mother's body.

Father never held her mother in front of him to shield himself. It was her mother's choice to sacrifice herself to save her father. *Grandfather lied. He lied to me! Why? For five years, he lied to me.* Then, her rage took over her mind.

***

Jayson and five others stopped outside Crystal's door. "Wait here until I call for you," Jayson ordered.

The door opened and closed behind Jayson, who saw the room in shambles. Crystal sat on her chair in the perfect pose of a young princess, her hands neatly grasped together on her lap. Jayson picked up the other chair off the floor and set it across from her.

Just as he sat on the chair, Crystal asked. "Why did Grandfather lie to me?"

Jayson studied her face, then answered, "Because he loved you. When your mother ran off and married your father, he was irate. Katherine was the youngest of his daughters and was the most loved. It was a great loss for my father and mother and the entire palace staff. Everyone loved Katherine. I'm sure I don't have to tell you that your mother was an extraordinary lady and mother to you. You have your mother's looks but not her personality. When you turned 17, my father convinced your mother that you should attend the local university to advance your education. Your grandfather had no intention of ever letting you go. You reminded grandfather too much of Katherine, and he lied to you about her death. With Mark out of the way, you were secured in his love. Now that you know the truth about Mark, will you tell me what is on your mind?"

"What can I say? My grandfather lied to me, and now he is dead." She paused and said, "No. Murdered." My mother died, and my father is missing off-world. There are multiple conspiracies to assassinate us, and my uncle has just told me I have a terrible character! What else would you like me to share with you, Uncle Jayson?"

"Crystal, life is never simple or easy, so I must send you away for your sake."

Before Crystal could react, Jayson pulled out a petite stunner and pulled the trigger. Jayson quickly caught and held her before she could fall to the floor.

"Come on in," Jayson shouted. As they were told to do beforehand, two men took Crystal and laid her on the bed. The third man set his case on the end table, removed a device, and placed it on her head. The third man hesitated, but Jayson broke in and said, "Go ahead, Doctor."

The king's family doctor replied, "You understand this is completely illegal?"

"What choice do we have?" said Jayson. "If it weren't for Terry, we would all be gone by now. With both the king and Terry gone, we are on borrowed time. Begin now, Doctor Shan."

Shan nodded his head and proceeded as instructed. After a few moments, the doctor removed the device from Crystal's head.

"You understand I can't guarantee that her real memory will be temporarily blocked or that the installed fault memory will be successful."

"It's the best we can do in the short timeframe," said Jayson.

"All right, ladies, it's your turn. We will wait outside the room."

One of the two ladies slipped a blue collar around Crystal's neck, a prisoner controller for non-compliant prisoners, and engaged the device. The other lady ordered the unconscious Crystal to stand up.

"Is the android ready for Crystal to be on the ship?" Jayson asked.

"Yes," the doctor replied, "she will be fully programmed as a nanny, and after a month, the android will say a commanded code word to remove the memory blockage."

"Where did you find the faulty memory?" Jayson asked.

"From a young lady close to Crystal's age and size. My daughter, Shelia."

Jayson thought back, as he had seen Shelia as she was standing next to Terry when the sniper hit them both.

"Shelia was critically injured; there wasn't anyone else on short notice with a false memory that would be suitable. Shortly after I copied her memory, Shelia died. But Crystal won't know that, so the memory of Shelia will live on," said the doctor.

Jayson placed his hand on the doctor's shoulder, "I am very sorry, Shan." Doctor Shan nodded his head.

"Find the guy who murdered my daughter."

"I promise he will be held accountable," said Jayson.

Both men turned toward the door as they heard it open. One of the ladies led Crystal out of her room, with the other following close behind her. Doctor Shan's face showed pain. "You ladies are very good at your job!"

Crystal's appearance had been changed by modifying her clothes and makeup. Crystal's sandy blond hair had been shortened and made brunette; her skin was darkened, and her blue eyes were now brown. The dress had been replaced with standard blue off-world coveralls. Crystal was now Doctor Shan's daughter, Shelia.

"What about the security gate?" Jayson asked.

"Her implant ID is registered as Shelia, and the semi-permanent contact lens has also been copied from Shelia's iris. Shelia's real body was removed before the coroner arrived at the palace's clinic. The coroner was told Shelia only received a minor injury and is resting at the doctor's home. When Crystal, now Shelia, arrives near the off-world security gate, the android will remove and dispose of the neck controller. Shelia's memory will take over, and she will recognize the android as her nanny."

"Where is her destination?" Shan asked.

"The Academy, headquarters of the Commonwealth Navy Security," Jayson replied. "I have a friend with the code to remove Crystal's memory block. When Crystal arrives in two weeks, she will meet up with her."

"Who is she? Can she be trusted?" Doctor Shan asked.

"She is my godmother's daughter, Sheba Steiner," Jayson replied.

Jayson was feeling very conscious of his bodyguard following him close by. The days of living a carefree lifestyle without looking over his shoulder were gone. With Terry gone, security was more uncertain than before. So far, keeping things under wraps has prevented mass panic, but for how long? The palace's security had kept things quiet. One suspected hitman had been arrested earlier, and he swallowed a pill that caused complete memory loss. The two others confirmed that the hitman was dead and had been using a phony identity. His family and relatives were now asking questions, and the truth would soon be open to the public. There was no question that this was an inside job, but who was behind all these assassinations?

In the mid-evening night, Jayson looked out the third-floor window and saw his four-year-old daughter, Jenny, in the garden courtyard by herself. "Come with me quickly!" said Jayson to his bodyguard. Jayson raced down the three-story stairway and ran down the far edge of the garden courtyard.

"Jenny, what are you doing here all alone?"

"Daddy, please don't scare my friend," said Jenny.

"What friend?" Jayson said as he looked over her shoulder and froze. It was a small black animal with a white stripe on its back—a hybrid earth skunk. Jayson forced himself to remain calm and said, "Jenny, maybe you should let the poor creature go."

"He is not poor. He is my best friend. I feed him every night before bedtime."

"How long have you been feeding him?" Jayson asked.

"Since last spring."

Jayson thought, *That was four months ago.* Now feeling relieved, he asked, "May I finish feeding him so that you can get ready for bed?"

"Well, okay. Here, you hold him."

Jayson clenched his teeth and held the tiny creature in his arms. "Take Jenny back to her mother. I will deal with this myself."

The bodyguard took Jenny's hand and walked her back to the palace. Jayson sat on the stone bench facing toward the palace. "Now, what will I do with you, little fellow?"

The creature snuggled and went to sleep in his arms while Jayson was thinking about how to set him free well away from here. Jayson glanced at the palace, then focused on a disturbing sight. Someone is inside my father's private locked den. Jayson looked down at the little creature and then back at the den window. The maids are going to hate me for this.

Fearful that the perpetrators may overhear him using the Comlink to call for backup, Jayson decided to handle this alone. He entered the palace, took the stairs to the third floor, turned right, and stopped at the fifth door. Jayson touched the wall switch and darkened the hallway lights. He manually touched the security pad settings, cracked the door, slapped the skunk on the head, threw it into the den, and locked the door.

Jayson stood back from the door with his stunner in his hand. He could hear a terrible racket taking place behind the door. He heard chairs and tables being moved, crashing noises, and screaming. The door flew open as the perpetrators fell out onto the hallway floor. Jayson fired his stunner, then turned on the hallway lights. With the left hand, Jayson held his nose to block the smell and looked at the intruder's face. "You!" said Jayson in disgust, then everything went black.

"Jayson, can you hear me?" The unknown voice seemed far away as Jayson was in semi-conscious awareness.

"Go away," Jayson whispered.

The voice said, "He heard me. Jayson, it is important that you wake up for your family's sake!"

Family. My family, thought Jayson. *What does my family have to do with this?*

"Honey, it's me, your wife, Jennifer. Please try to pull through."

Jennifer, I must pull through. She needs me. I've got to pull through! "Ack, my head. Where am I?" cried Jayson.

"You're in the hospital," said Doctor McGee.

Jayson looked around, and sure enough, he was in the hospital.

"What am I doing here?" Jayson asked.

"We were hoping you could tell us," said Doctor Shan. "All we know from the burnt hair at the back of your head is that someone held and fired a stunner at your head. You are very lucky to be alive!"

Jayson, dazed, asked, "Where did this happen?"

"In the hallway outside your father's private den," said Jennifer.

"Hallway. Den." Then Jayson sat up and fell back on the bed.

"Take it easy, Jayson. Move slowly so that the dizziness doesn't overwhelm you."

Jayson slowly sat up but did not feel the usual hour-long effects of the stunner wearing off.

"How long have I been unconscious?"

"About four hours since we found you on the hallway floor," Jennifer replied.

Four hours. A lot can happen in four hours.

"Do you remember what happened?" the doctor asked.

"No, I can't. Wait, maybe I can. Someone broke into Father's den; I stunned him, but there must have been another one in the den because when I looked down on the body, I lost consciousness."

"Do you remember who it was?" Shan asked.

"I thought so at first, but now I can't remember," Jayson replied. "What else can you tell me, Shan?"

"Our security said that whoever it was, one of them was very powerful. It is clear that he carried the body out of the palace, broke the guard's neck, and ripped out the cam's recorder. And just so you know, the local authorities are waiting outside to interview you. One of them is a Commonwealth agent, too. The whole country knows now what has happened at the palace."

"I've sure made a stink of everything, haven't I, Shan?"

"I assume you mean the skunk," the doctor laughed.

"Jenny told me about the skunk, and I was horrified that no one has been aware of it for four months," Jennifer retorted.

Jayson sighed, "I suppose you should let the authorities interview me."

Shan nodded his head.

***

"Jayson, please try to relax," Jennifer pleaded.

"How can I when we are under house arrest? The palace is on lockdown, and both the local and the Commonwealth authorities are searching for something they refuse to explain.

The government also violated the constitution, claiming they represent the New Order of the people. Don't they understand the repercussions of ignoring the Opposition Party and other factions?"

"At least the present government allowed us to live in our cottage."

"That they did," Jayson sighed.

"Lord Jayson," the android butler announced, "An inspector of the palace's chief of staff is here to speak with you."

Who could that be? It must be Terry's replacement, Jayson thought. A solidly built man as tall as himself with brown crew-cut hair walked into the family guest room. *I should have known Terry's right-hand man, Mr. Jonesborough.*

"Inspector Jonesborough, what can I do for you other than congratulate you on your promotion?"

Jonesborough grunted and replied, "Just doing my job, Jayson. Could we speak in private? Maybe outside on the garden patio?"

"Go ahead, Jayson. I will check on Jenny," Jennifer said as she exited the guest room.

"After you, Jayson," said the inspector.

Why do I have a nagging feeling about this man? Jayson thought. He led the inspector to a private patio and sat on the cast-iron chair.

The inspector stood and said, "Sorry for my rude suggestion, but this patio is the only safe area; I couldn't find a cam or bug. Please understand that I am on your side."

"And you show this by placing my family and me under house arrest, Inspector?"

The inspector smiled, "So you already know. Yes, that is quite true. However, if I hadn't, you would be behind bars for suspicion of murder and unauthorized interference in a crime scene."

"But I have that authority!" Jayson protested.

"The present government has dissolved the monarchy and is building a case against you. From what I have heard, your father refused to abdicate the throne when he turned 80. The bitterness and friction between the two of you caused things to get out of control. They're accusing you of murder, or I should say multiple murders. Of course, it's all a lie, and they know it, but having you out of the way is necessary to complete their agenda. You could successfully fight back, and should that happen, an accident could be a more convenient option."

Jayson suddenly felt tired, "Then what am I to do?"

"Go off-world," replied the inspector. "Your father's yacht is still available and is manned by his crew, who are loyal toward you. I can help you and your family discreetly escape from here to your father's ship by night. Once your family is on board, it's up to you to decide on the destination."

"I have to think about this!"

"You have only five days to agree to this plan, or it will be too late. The prosecutor will be ready to lay charges against you in five days."

The inspector pulled his gloves and said, "It will be a chilly night."

One of the gloves slipped from his hand and fell to the patio's stone surface. Jayson bent down to pick up the glove, and the lost memory flooded back into his mind. Jayson stared at the glove and handed it back to the inspector.

"Very well. I will prepare to leave in the next three days."

The inspector nodded his head and turned away to leave.

***

"Off-warp jump begins in 5, 4, 3, 2, 1. We are now in regular space, Liz," the pilot announced.

The bridge was quiet for a minute; then, the captain breathed. "I think we are safe, Jayson."

"Liz, prepare us for the next warp jump."

"Yes, Captain," said Liz. "Ship Computer, calculate the next destination."

"While we are waiting, let's go to my quarters," said the captain.

"After you, Captain," Jayson said as he followed.

When the captain sat in his chair, he collected his thoughts momentarily, then asked, "Let's start at the beginning again. When and where did you get your memory back?"

Jayson cleared his throat and spoke in monotone, "The inspector made one unfortunate mistake. The inspector neglected to remove the skunk smell from the glove he had on him. When I picked it up from the ground, the skunk smell triggered my missing memory, and I now remember everything outside my father's den. The man on the floor was none other than Inspector Jonesborough. I also knew right then that the escape plan is a setup."

"But you decided to continue with the plan?"

"What else could I do? It's my word against his, and there is more than one faction against me. Life has become very cheap, and I fear for my family. Not to mention, who is the unknown person who nearly killed me with the stunner at the back of my head."

"How did you survive that attack?" the captain asked.

"I must have turned my head just enough to receive a hard knockout instead of a direct hit. Otherwise, you are correct; I would not be talking to you now."

"How did you know about the bomb hidden aboard my ship?"

"I didn't. However, it was simply too easy to have the yacht ready for me, so I passed the message on to you to check for any explosives before we went off-world."

"Ted, where did you find the bomb?"

"We almost didn't find it. The bomb was hidden in the drive end with a smart timer set to go off in warp space."

"Do you know who planted the bomb?" Jayson asked.

"Yes. Our cam shows that one of our relief engineer technicians was responsible, but he is back on Planet New Sweoland. Jayson, it's good that you came when you did, as the authorities were about to throw us all out of work and seize my ship."

"Sometimes, Ted, timing is all God's good work," Jayson smiled.

The captain shook his head in agreement.

"One more question. Why did you pick our new destination?"

"The inspector knew I would decide on Father's resort, a three-day journey at warp speed. The resort is out of the local authorities' jurisdiction, and no treaty exists between them. When I heard the Commonwealth authorities were involved in the investigation, I knew the resort would not be a safe place for us."

"Twenty-five years ago, I had a one-year contract with an old friend, Captain Mark Styler of the ship *Marvel*. Mark was a ship owner and operator merchant trader."

"He was your brother-in-law?" the captain asked.

"Yes, Mark married my youngest sister, Katherine, who is Crystal's mother. Part of our agreement during the one-year contract was that Mark would teach me the merchant trade and how to make contract agreements. At the end of the contract, I was to recommend my replacement. Unknown to Mark, my replacement was my sister Katy, and one year later, they decided to get married. As for our destination, our four-week journey will take us to Midway, a solid iron 3034-mile-wide asteroid considered a dwarf planet between Sector Two and the territory of Sector Five. The Commonwealth hasn't set up a traffic control there yet, and we can keep a low profile near one of the frontier outposts. I have a contact at the outpost who can help us change the ship register. Then, we can plan our next move."

"This contact of yours, this person can be trusted?" Ted asked.

"Yes, I know she can be trusted."

***

Chapter 3

The Year 2390

Alone in a dim room, two Navy Security military personnel sat across each other: Rear Admiral T.A. Melnyk, a tall, daunting man, and Commodore Doctor Halley, a man with a heavy physique and medium height.

"Admiral, are you sure you can go ahead with this?"

"If the boys upstairs find out about this, I'm done as Rear Admiral."

"It's not your fault that Steiner stuck her nose where it didn't belong."

"It's more than that; I'm guilty by association. We had an affair thirty years ago when Sheba was only an ensign media technician. An affair between a commander and an ensign is grounds for a court-martial."

"That was a long time ago, Admiral. What proof could she have that you two had an affair?"

"A 28-year-old son. When Tom was born 28 years ago, the doctors performed the usual physiological and psychological examinations and found that Tom had a rare mental disorder. He lacks a filter between his conscious and subconscious mind. The doctor has concluded that as Tom gets older, he will develop a schizophrenia-like syndrome. This mental disorder is characterized by abnormal social behavior and a failure to understand reality. Common symptoms include false beliefs, unclear or confused thinking, hearing voices that others do not, and reduced social engagement and emotional expression. People with schizophrenia often have additional mental health problems such as anxiety, depression, or substance use disorders."

"It is now well documented that there are filtering processes between the conscious and subconscious elements of the mind. This research on neurologically impaired individuals demonstrates beyond any shadow of a doubt that there is an 'interpreter' housed in the left hemisphere of the brain that reports on what the person is doing and why. This aspect of consciousness can be functionally isolated from other mental processes. A committee was organized to determine the best steps to take to build the necessary brain cells when Tom ages."

"Did the doctors start the cellular construction?" Halley asked.

"Yes," Melnyk replied. "But his mother was convinced that an inconvenient accident would remove Tom from his existence. That would certainly help my case. Sheba took Tom away to an off-world planet to find someone to help with his condition. Her network of local and off-world friends arranged for them to settle on Sector Three, Solar System Sunna, and Planet New Sweoland. They began their medical procedure for Tom in secret—or so they thought."

"You knew all along about their undercover operations?" Halley asked.

Melnyk replied, "Of course, that's my job as Navy Security, and this is how we operate. Sheba and her friends are decent at covering their tracks but not good enough. Informally, the Stevenson family is run by the Monarch Royalty Society and is semi-independent from the Commonwealth. Sheba had a close relationship with the king and his family in the past and obtained protection from the Commonwealth authorities."

"Did the doctors perform any cellular construction on Tom's mind at that time?" Halley asked.

"Almost," Melnyk replied. "A year after their arrival, Tom was lying on his bed with a window open nearby. Lightning struck the window, hit Tom's bed, and grazed his head. He was in a coma for five days before awakening. The medical treatment was postponed until the doctors could understand Tom's predicament."

"What was his diagnosis?" Halley asked.

"The doctors were flabbergasted. Tom's schizophrenia was cured, but they realized something else had taken place in his brain. Tom's mind could separate direct contact between his conscious and subconscious minds for the next three years of observation. However, whenever Tom requested information he could not comprehend, his subconscious provided the answer."

"I am not surprised, as the subconscious part of the mind is ten times bigger and faster than the conscious mind," said Halley, who paused and asked, "What happened afterward?"

"With a medical certificate saying that Tom is normal, they returned to the Academy, and Sheba raised Tom as a single mother."

"And they lived happily ever after," Halley added.

"Not really," Melnyk replied. "Tom never had a male role model for his emotional well-being, as Sheba never had a stable relationship with a man throughout these years. Tom became introverted during his younger and teen years and started to rebel. He was a computer nerd with a network of friends with similar odd traits. Sheba was concerned for her son and turned to help from one of the local ministers. They turned their life around in a short time when they let God into their life. Tom entered university and completed a six-year computer science program in four years. Then, I received a call from Sheba." Melnyk paused and continued, "She blackmailed me into hiring Tom as a private subcontractor and cryptologic technician. I have to give her credit; Sheba's got the guts and smarts to confront me," Melnyk grinned.

"Is that safe?" Halley said, alarmed.

"I didn't have much choice in the matter. I had to accept it either or face a court martial. Surprisingly, for the last six years, Tom has proven to be an excellent operator, as nothing escapes his attention. He is probably the best the Navy Security has ever hired."

"A week ago, Sheba confronted me with her discovery of my direct involvement in the missing ship *Marvel*. I had no choice but to use my agents to arrest her."

"What's so important about the *Marvel*?"

"I am not privileged to explain that to you."

"All right, so what is the next step?" Halley asked.

"A permanent mind wipe, a new false identity, and sending her far away from here. To one of the off-world outposts."

"Can we get away with this?" Halley asked.

The rear admiral said dryly, "She isn't the first person the Commonwealth Navy Security has dealt with before. Besides, conducting these types of operations is your expertise."

"What about this son of yours?"

"For now, nothing," Melnyk replied.

***

"Hey, Tom, wait up!" Tom Steiner stopped and waited for his girlfriend to catch up with him.

"Where are you going? I thought we were going to spend time together after work."

"Didn't you get my messages, Sharon?"

"I'm Sorry, Tom. There's a lot of commotion with security, and I've been too busy."

"Same here. I put in a double shift in the past two days."

"Do you know what's going on?" Sharon asked.

"You know I can't talk about these things," Tom said, slightly annoyed. "Besides, my mother wanted me to pick up a friend at the port. Mother said she got a hot lead on her story and won't be able to pick up her friend. Look, Sharon, I have to get going, or I'll be late."

"How about tomorrow, then?" Sharon asked.

"Tomorrow it is," Tom replied.

Sharon smiled and gave Tom a quick hug. "See you later," she said as she rushed in the opposite direction.

Tom sighed and continued to the nearest taxi. At the off-world spaceport lobby, he watched as the crowd exited the security area. The last to exit the security area was a typical gray-skinned bio-artificial android and a young woman. She was a pleasant-looking, tall, dark-haired woman. She was light-tanned and much younger than he thought. *They must be the two my mother was waiting for*, Tom thought.

"Are you Shelia McGee?" Tom asked.

"Yes, I am, but who are you?"

"My name is Tom Steiner. My mother's name is Sheba Steiner, and she could not come to meet you here. Mother asked me to take her place instead."

"May I see your I.D., please?" the android broke in.

"This is Manny, my nanny."

"Certainly," Tom said as he downloaded his I.D. to Manny from his implant.

"Your identification has been received and verified. Thank you," said Manny.

"Is this all your possessions?" Tom saw only two small bags.

"We were planning to do some shopping after we arrived here at the Academy."

Tom shrugged, "All right, I have a taxi on standby outside."

With the three of them inside the taxi, they flew toward the private apartment on the city's outskirts. The elevator took them to the third floor, and they entered Sheba's flat.

"It looks like Mother is still not home. Shelia, your bedroom will be the first to the left and the first to the right for you, Manny. I will be in Mother's office to see if there are any messages."

Tom checked to see any messages but was disappointed to find his inbox empty. This was unsurprising, as his mother often kept a low profile when investigating a good story. But something was bothering him, and he couldn't put his finger on it. Tom left his mother's office and saw Shelia resting on the couch making herself at home.

"Can I get you anything?" Tom asked.

"No, thank you. Manny will get it for me."

"Where is she now?" he asked, as he could not see the android in the apartment living room.

"In her room connecting with the terminal. She is checking all the stores and restaurants. Have you heard anything from your mother yet?"

"Nothing," Tom sighed, hoping to hear from his mother soon. "How did you get to know my mother?"

"That is strange. I can't remember."

Tom felt a little alarmed, then asked, "Why are you here, then?"

Shelia shrugged her shoulders with her hands up in the air.

Tom got annoyed by the girl's answers when Manny interrupted him. "It's true; she doesn't know why she is here."

"And I suppose you do?" Tom asked.

"To a limited degree," Manny replied. "Your mother, Sheba, is a friend of Lord Jayson Stevenson."

"Lord? Do you mean to say a royal family member?" Tom asked.

"Yes, Lord Jayson made a personal request for your mother to assist young Shelia for an uncertain time."

"Then Shelia is a princess?" Tom said as he looked sideways at Shelia.

"No. Shelia is Doctor Shan McGee's daughter, a private doctor of the king, and a friend to Lord Jayson. When we arrived at the orbit station yesterday morning, I forwarded Lord Jayson's messages to your mother."

Tom remembered when Mother had asked him to assist Shelia and Manny. He sat across from Shelia, "That still doesn't answer my question. Why are you both here?"

"I do not know. You will have to ask your mother," said Shelia.

"Okay. We have to wait for my mother to arrive. It's also dinner time. Shelia, would you like me to make something for you?"

"That won't be necessary; Manny will make something for me."

"Well, if you will excuse me, my flat is just down the hallway on the left side from here. Just use my mother's door com-link if you need me. I will be back in an hour or two."

As he exited his mother's flat, Tom was glad to be out and away from Shelia. He entered his flat and asked the room's computer, "Are there any messages for me?"

"None," the computer replied. Tom grabbed a protein bar from the kitchen and sat on his couch with his feet on the living room coffee table. The odd feeling returned and began to bother him again, more vital than ever. Tom's photographic memory and his perfectionism made him look around to see what was different in the living room. His hair was raised on the back of his head when he realized the picture on the wall ledge was at a slightly wrong angle. *Someone has to be in this room*, Tom thought.

Tom calmly picked up his notepad and touched the screen to make the home page appear. He discreetly touched the home security icon; words appeared stating that there had been no security breaches. Tom closed the app and touched a different hidden icon: a backup security cam.

The notepad said, "Warning, the premises have been breached!" Tom watched two individuals enter his flat: one entered his office while the other searched the rest of the rooms. They both used a scanner Tom recognized. They were very careful not to touch anything. The cam shifted to his office, where one of the men used his scanner to download the memory data from his computer. Then, he took a mini cam from his shirt pocket and placed it on the back of the glass photo near the computer terminal. The cam would also monitor the computer.

Tom's notepad shifted back to the living room to see the other man who had set a cam behind the photo on the wall's ledge. The door opened, and Tom was shocked as he saw Sharon!

"Time is up, guys," Sharon said. "Let's go now. Did you touch anything here?"

"No, but what's the big deal about touching anything?"

"Tom has a photographic memory, which is part of why he is so good at his job as a cryptologic technician. He doesn't miss anything."

"Did you finish with Sheba's flat?" one of the men asked.

"Same as here; one cam in the office and the other in the living room. We've got five minutes left to leave this building before the security is back in service."

"We've finished with this place," said the other man. "Our people will analyze the data I have collected."

"All right. Let's go," Sharon said. I've got an hour before I meet up with Tom."

When the trio left his flat, Tom closed his eyes and sighed. Tom opened his eyes, gently turned off his notepad, and set it back on the end table. Mindful of the spy cam facing him, he walked to the kitchen to ponder his troubling revelations.

Tom considered his predicament while eating his leftovers. *My mother's and my computer terminals are not secure, but it may be possible that my computer at the Navy headquarters is not yet bugged. I will have to risk it, as it may be the only way to get to the bottom of this.*

After cleaning the kitchen, Tom returned to his mother's flat and announced himself at the door's com-link. Manny stood before him as the door slid open.

"Please inform Shelia that I have unfinished work at the office and will see her in the morning. Hopefully, by then, we will have heard from my mother." Without waiting for a response, Tom turned away, walked down the aisle, and left the building.

Tom knew he couldn't bypass the main headquarters' security. Instead, he entered the Navy Security building in the usual manner. The computer security allowed Tom in without difficulties, a sign that his office may not be monitored yet. One of the perks of working as a highly regarded privately hired cryptologic technician for the Commonwealth Navy Security was having an office to yourself with no distractions. Here, Tom could be hyper-focused on his assignments. Considering that the room may have a hidden bug, Tom followed the usual procedure. He removed his jacket, made his coffee, checked the latest official news, and turned on the computer terminal.

His three monitors lit up before him. Tom started where he had left off earlier in the day and risked being caught in the act as he discreetly inserted a memory disc in the receiver. A hologram lit up before him on another monitor, a ghost program independent of the Navy's constant monitoring of his computer station.

Tom smiled, just like he had in the old days, ten years before, as an unknown computer hacker. When his mother discovered Tom's talents, she made him turn his back on life as a hacker, and with the help of his father's influence in the Navy, he became a top-notch cryptologic technician. *There is no doubt my mother blackmailed him to hire me on with the Navy Security*, he grinned.

Okay, let's find out who this Sharon is. Tom slipped inside the back door of the Navy personal records and entered Sharon's full name. "RESTRICTED," the computer replied. *No problem*, Tom thought. He took the back door to the restricted records and read the data. *Whoa, did Sharon ever fool me*, thought Tom. *Sharon's real name is Grace Morrison, and she's twice my age. The Navy must have spent a lot to keep her looking young. With the human 120-year lifespan, our appearance stops aging at 35 to 40 years. Sharon looks only 25. One of Sharon's significant assignments is to keep an eye on me.*

Tom felt annoyed that his relationship with Sharon was a farce. *So why am I the focus of the Navy's security? Who ordered the assignment? Wait, what are Sharon's other assignments?*

Surprised by the long list of assignments he read about, Tom stopped when his mother's name, Sheba Steiner, appeared. There was no cross-reference to who ordered the assignment, except that it came from a Navy Security department Tom had never heard of before. Tom searched each of the 24 bloated Navy Security departments for the sub-department mentioned in Sharon's records. After searching the eighteenth department, Tom found it. He entered the site, copied what he needed, and exited quickly, hoping to avoid the tight security.

Tom covered his tracks as he exited his terminal and looked at the clock above him on the wall. Two hours passed, but he continued with his usual assignment before shutting down. He removed his disc and slipped it into his hidden pocket.

Tom stood up, washed his cup, put on his jacket, and left the office. The cool air outside helped clear his mind of the data overload. Both Tom and his mother were being watched. *Who is this, Shelia? What am I going to do about Sharon, or is it Grace? That is the hardest one to answer. Is Sharon responsible for Mother's possible disappearance? What do I say to Sharon, "Hey Sharon, I heard you are a spy,"* Tom thought dryly. *Tomorrow is our weekend off work. How am I to be comfortable with Sharon while Shelia is around? I will have to deal with it as if nothing has happened and play the game until later. In the meantime, I should find out what is on the memory disc and get some sleep.*

***

"What do you think, Tom?" Shelia was standing nearby with a new dress for the 12th time! Tom had to admit, though, that it did look good on her. Sharon was standing beside Tom with her arms across her chest.

"That's the best one yet," Sharon said with a smile.

"Wonderful!" said Shelia. "I have two more dresses to try out," she said as she rushed to the changing room. "Thanks for helping us out with Shelia in shopping for her clothes," Tom said to Sharon.

"Shopping with the girls is much fun!" Sharon said as she hugged Tom's arm. "And with my favorite guy, too!" She became slightly tense when she didn't see a smile reflected in Tom's eyes, "Is there something wrong, Tom?"

"Sorry. I worked overtime yesterday at the office to finish my assignment. I didn't realize we would be shopping the next day."

Sharon's eyes widened when she recognized someone near the corner of the walkway outside the store's glass wall. Sharon quickly composed herself and said, "Could you take over? I need to find the washroom."

Without waiting for an answer, Sharon hurried out the side entrance of the open mall. She walked toward the back of a thin young man, stuck her thumb in his throat, and forcefully shoved him into the women's washroom nearby. Sharon slammed him against the wall and said, "You idiot. Why are you spying on us, Ted?"

Ted coughed from his injured throat. "I am not spying; I have a message for you."

"You could have texted me instead," Sharon said angrily.

"I have my orders not to use any communications."

"Who sent you?" Sharon demanded.

In a panic, Ted said, "Eric. I mean Fox!"

Sharon rolled her eyes, "I can't believe this," she muttered. "What are the messages from Fox?" Sharon asked.

"I am to tell you the code word 'Maccabee'."

"Okay, you are off the hook this time, but let this be very clear—Tom is no dummy; you could have blown my cover. Tell Fox that if he ever sends you again, the local authorities will find your body in the sewer. Now get along, Ted!"

Maccabee...something big is going on with the Navy Security, Sharon thought. I've got one hour to get to the inner committee circle at headquarters. Sharon took a big breath and exited the washroom.

"Hey, Tom. I'm not feeling well. Would you mind spending the rest of the day helping Shelia without me? Thanks!" Without another word, Sharon left with a huff.

Feeling relieved by Sharon's sudden departure, Tom heard Shelia say, "Last dress for you to look at," as she smiled.

For someone so obnoxious, she does have a pretty smile, thought Tom. "I like it; it suits you."

"Good. I am finished with the dresses and shoes. When we are back home, Manny will have dinner ready for us. I will arrange to have my merchandise delivered to our flat."

"Shelia, there's one more thing I want to do before we head home. I want to pick up some electronic parts at the supplier nearby."

Shelia hugged Tom's arm and said, "All right. I'll come with you."

Tom was unsure whether he should be annoyed or pleased that Shelia held his arm as they walked to the supplier a block away.

"Here we are," Tom said as they entered the supply store.

"If you don't mind, I will look around while you get your stuff," said Shelia.

Tom approached one of the clerks, Andy Liu, who was standing behind the parts counter. "Hello, Andy."

"Hi, Tom. I will be right back." Tom looked around to see what Shelia was up to, and he noticed her keen interest in the various electronic parts on display at the storefront.

"Here is your stuff, Tom."

"Thanks for holding them for me. I owe you for this, Andy."

"Forget it, Tom. That's what friends are for. Who is your lady over there?"

"Her name is Shelia, and she is a friend of my mother." They could hear her helping out a customer with her advice.

"This component has a three-to-one lifespan over the other competitor."

"It looks like Shelia knows what she is talking about," Andy smiled.

Tom, impressed, nodded his head.

"See you around, Andy," Tom said as he took his bags.

When Tom was outside, he asked, "How did you know about all that back there with the customer?"

Shelia paused and stared blankly, "I don't know; I just know," then laughed. "Never mind. It's time to head home. I'm getting hungry."

Puzzled by Shelia's answer, Tom decided to leave it for now and agreed that it was time to head home.

***

"Thanks for dinner, Shelia, and you too, Manny. I am going to call it a night. After the Gospel meeting tomorrow morning, do you want to walk in the city park?"

"Are you a Christian?" Shelia asked.

"Yes, I am, and so is my mother."

"What about your father?"

"I don't know my father very well, but he has no time for God. My mother didn't want anything to do with my birth father, and he didn't show much interest in me. I was a loner until Sharon became a friend a few years ago."

"Are you and Sharon close friends?" Shelia smiled.

She does have a pretty smile, Tom thought. "Right now, I'm not so sure," Tom replied. "Well, good night," Tom said as he exited the kitchen chair.

As Tom was leaving, Shelia said, "I'll go!"

"What?" Tom asked.

"I would like to walk down to the park with you."

"Okay, I will meet you here before noon," Tom smiled.

While in bed, Tom took a digital reader from the bag he had picked up from the supplier. He inserted the memory disc he had copied from the office in the reader, which the camera couldn't pick up in the office or living room. After 10 minutes,

Tom found what he was looking for: the one who had ordered the investigation into him and his mother. The code name was Bear, otherwise known as Rear Admiral T.S. Melnyk, his father.

Chapter 4

A short walking distance from the city boundaries were many different parks known for their specific cultural environments, which the automatic mower and android gardeners maintained. Tom and Shelia walked along the many sporadic trails throughout the treeless park. Shelia looked down from a low hill and saw a slow-moving river nearby that flowed from the city.

"This is a good spot, Tom. Let's have our picnic here."

Tom unfolded the blanket from his backpack as they sat down. "What did you bring for lunch?"

"Manny made some sandwiches for us," Shelia replied.

Manny again, Tom thought dryly. *Doesn't she do anything for herself?* "Do you have a favorite park back home?" Tom asked.

"There are a few parks I enjoyed; one was at the palace, and the other was where my mother died when I was barely a toddler."

"What happened to your mother?"

"I am not sure. How strange, I can't remember," Shelia was puzzled by her lack of memories. She continued, "The palace is on a low hilltop overlooking a small lake. There is a six-step terrace of garden plants down the slope from the palace toward the lake. The garden consists of many marble benches, fountains, patios, statues, ornate pole lamps, and a few small furry animals."

"How did you manage to live in the palace?"

"My father had been assigned as a private doctor for the royal Stevenson family, which is how I got to know one of my best friends, Crystal." Shelia felt odd; her face flushed red, and she had a blank expression.

"Is there something wrong?" Tom looked concerned.

"I don't … not sure. Let's walk, please! What is that?" Shelia said as she pointed at a distant dark pattern in the open sky.

"Help me clean up, and I can show you," Tom suggested. They quickly folded the blanket and put the lunch back in his backpack. Tom grabbed Shelia's hand. "Let's hurry, or we will be too late to find a good bench."

Tom and Shelia ran down the garden path toward the slow waterway. The garden path opened up along the river, where many benches were located. "We are in luck. Over there is an empty bench for us." Just as they were about to sit on the bench, another couple cut in, protesting.

"Hey, lady, move along. We want this bench." Shelia looked up to face an enormous man standing over her.

Shelia stood her ground and crossed her arms. "I don't think so, Buster; we got here first," she replied.

"In my opinion…" the man said.

Shelia interrupted the man, "If you have an opinion, please raise your right hand. Now put it over your mouth."

The man's girlfriend cut in, "Let's go, Honey. I think she has a mental illness!"

Shelia responded, "Actually, I enjoy it," she smiled.

"I think you're right. Let's move on," the man said.

Tom struggled not to laugh, "You sure know how to hold your ground. Those guys backed off quickly! Here they come," Tom shouted.

"What?" Shelia asked.

"The birds' mating season is about to start," Tom replied.

Shelia looked upstream toward the city and saw a massive flock of birds flying low above the river.

"Look down the other way," Tom advised.

Shelia looked downstream and saw another flock of birds coming. As the birds flew closer, she noticed the birds' white feathers, each with a striped orange underbelly, wings, and a long tail. When thousands of birds emerged in pairs, they spiraled up several hundred feet in the air. One of the birds in each pair wrapped its wings over its partner's body as both birds fell into the river. Just before they hit the river, the birds flew apart to try again. The mating performance continued for 30 minutes, and the birds flew off in pairs toward the ocean.

"Where are they going?" Shelia asked.

"There is a bird sanctuary on an island a few miles out," Tom said.

Tom was suddenly aware that Shelia had snuggled up and was holding his arm.

"That was so beautiful. Thank you for bringing me here. It was so romantic how those birds flew away in pairs. Let's finish eating our lunch," said Shelia.

"Were you planning to marry a prince on a white horse at the palace someday?" Tom asked.

"No. I wanted a weirdo who could make me laugh."

Tom couldn't help but smile at Shelia. *She's one complex lady. One moment, she is a polite girl. Next, she is a sarcastic woman.*

"Have you heard from your mother?" Shelia asked.

"No, but that's okay. My mother usually is gone for three or four days when she has a good story."

"It seems that most people here work for the Navy, as many are dressed in military uniform," said Shelia.

"Academy is the newest military outpost and the most important Navy Security outpost in the Commonwealth's four sectors. Most private citizens have worked for the Navy at one time or another. Many have quit, retired, and gone private, like my mother."

"What did she do?" Shelia asked.

"She was mainly in the Navy media division, but after my mother had a short affair with my birth father, she quit the Navy and got a job with the local media station."

"How about you, Tom?"

"I am a private contractor connected with the Navy Security. I work on special assignments. I can't explain for security-related reasons."

"That's all right, I understand. I must pay heed to many security-related issues back at the palace," said Shelia.

"Shelia, I have to go back to work tomorrow. Are you and Manny going to be all right by yourself this week?"

"Manny will think of something to occupy me."

Manny again, Tom rolled his eyes. "Are you tired?" Tom asked.

"No, let's walk along the river back to town."

Tom smiled and shook his head.

***

Tom was tired, but as he finished his assignments near the end of the day, he began to think about Shelia. *Why not*, Tom thought. He entered Shelia's name and home world, and an image of Shelia appeared on the monitor; it was a younger photo of Shelia by five years. The data covered her status, medical records, family, and education.

Tom had the odd feeling that he was missing something important. He hyper-focused on the monitor and found it: the trademark icon representing a top-secret investigation into the monarchy and the Stevenson family.

It looks interesting. Should I risk it? Tom thought. *Go for it!* He inserted his disc in the receiver. A separate screen appeared, and he began his search for the new icon. *This is odd; I have never seen this before. Maybe I should back off and get out*, Tom thought. *I've gotten this far. It's too late to quit now.*

The site was entirely of security blocks, which made Tom more determined to find what data was hidden. *Here's the 'top-secret' manuscript!* he thought. *It takes a lot of educated guesses to figure out what the icon might be. Could it have been keeping secrets through cryptology?* Tom used what is called an expectancy-intensification algorithm. Instead of relying on a predefined vocabulary, the algorithm would run through every possible English translation of those foreign words, no matter how ridiculous.

Tom spoke in a near whisper yet with intensity and passion. He made mental notes on the coded pages in his memory implant. *Unfortunately, there is much work to do next.* For an hour, he went through the cipher, developing a scheme to transcribe the coded script into easy-to-type, machine-readable text. *This is not random. I can crack this one,* he told himself. As long as he could learn some basic rules about the language, his subconscious would lead him each step of the way. Tom still hadn't cracked the code, but his hand had a life of its own through his subconscious mind.

Even with some of the code broken, the swirl of ritual and double-talk was getting easier to follow, especially for someone with years of hacking experience during his younger days. Usually, it concerned new rites of bloodlines of the political order, while others detailed political movements. There was no way to tell because they were cryptologically sealed, with a secret history of the Commonwealth's four sectors waiting to be revealed.

It even has a virus! Tom isolated the virus, locked it onto his disc, and downloaded the encrypted data. He followed the protocol before exiting the computer station. He felt relief from something too deep for him to understand genuinely, yet he felt justified in his action. *Now, why do I think that?* Tom took the disc from the receiver and returned it to his concealed pouch. *It's time to go home.*

When Tom walked beyond the null shield surrounding the Navy Security building, his com-link was reactivated. A voice message alerted him. It was from Sharon; she had been notified to report for duty and would be in touch later today or tomorrow. Tom felt more relieved than disappointed and headed home. Then, he thought better and walked to the electronics supply store. Andy was just about to close the store when Tom entered.

Relieved that they were alone, Tom asked, "Andy, I need something from you."

"Like?" said Andy.

"An up-to-date decoder."

"That's risky, Tom."

"I know, but it's important; otherwise, I would not ask for it."

Andy thought about it and said, "There are two conditions: I want it back tomorrow, and I want something from you."

"What is it?" Tom asked.

"Rumours are something big is going on with the Navy."

"I haven't heard, but I will look into it," said Tom.

"Good, wait here," Andy said as he went to the back room. A short time later, he returned with a bag and set it on the counter. This decoder had two buttons: "Black to engage, red for the meltdown, in case you get caught."

"Understood," Tom said as he placed the device in his backpack.

Later that night, after Tom discreetly checked his room for any new evidence of disturbances or added bugs, he removed the decoder. He inserted the memory disc from his concealed pocket. After a few minutes, the decoder released the disc, and Tom inserted it back into his private reader. For the next hour, Tom was fascinated by what the data revealed. The complete backgrounds of all the royal members were listed: their history, government ships, rivals, and political corruption.

The data had a good breakdown of the royal Stevenson family, but why the investigation? Tom opened the following icon, and his eyes opened wide. After Tom had finished, he removed the disc and put it back in his pocket. Tom was up most of the night, kept awake by the disturbing information he had gathered from the investigation.

The Commonwealth Navy Security knew about the bomb on the royal yacht and did nothing about it. Lord Jayson was either dead or missing, Shelia was Crystal with a blocked memory, Inspector Jonesborough was a drug-induced sleeping agent with an "unknown controller," and people had been murdered.

The Commonwealth Security had stepped back and turned a blind eye to the whole matter. The worst news was saved for last: the man who was in charge of the investigation was none other than his father. *Why?* Tom thought, dismayed by the whole affair. *Just who am I working for?* Tom's spirit was deeply troubled by these thoughts.

It wasn't until 5 am that he finally fell asleep. An hour later, the alarm clock woke Tom, and with a grunt, he forced himself to wake up with a pounding migraine. "I hope this isn't a virus," Tom muttered. *VIRUS, I forgot about the security virus.* Tom returned to his bedroom and reinserted the memory disc to the reader.

Tom studied the virus. *Oh, am I ever lucky?* he thought. My cover was nearly blown. This is one intelligent virus. If I go back to this site, they will be ready for me and will be able to track me down. My ghost program will be unable to hide me from detection.

The door charm buzzed and announced, "Sharon Giezer."

Sharon! What is she doing here? Tom sighed and said, "Open."

Sharon stood at the door entrance, "I am sorry for the no-show yesterday, but I have to run. I am going off-world and don't know when I will be back."

"What's going on with the Navy? Another war coming up?"

Sharon was about to answer but then thought better of it and asked, "Tom, have you been sleeping okay? You've got bags under your eyes."

"I woke up with a migraine; it has been a long night. I know, I should have taken the sleep aid."

Sharon stared at Tom momentarily and said, "Tom, I have to go now." Then, she whispered, "Be careful and trust no one." Before Tom could speak, Sharon turned on her heels, quickly walked down the hallway, and exited the door.

Tom still had mixed feelings about Sharon. *Can I trust her?* His migraine made it hard to think, and he took some meds from the medicine cabinet. In a few minutes, his migraine was gone. *I might drop the decoder back to Andy before heading to work.* When Tom caught up with Andy at the store, he acted professionally, knowing something was wrong.

"How long will it take for you to fix my reader," he said as he returned the decoder to Andy.

"Sorry. I won't have time for it today."

"Okay, I'll come back later." Tom left with alarming knowledge: the building was under surveillance! *This is not good news; I'd better watch myself.* When Tom arrived early at the Navy Center for work, he saw military security police blocking the main entrance.

"I'm sorry, but these premises are locked down today. Didn't you receive the notice 30 minutes ago?"

"I left home an hour ago, and my com-link seems to be shut down."

"We shut down all personal communications," the policeman said.

"What's going on here?" Tom asked.

"Security breach is all I can tell you, so you might as well go home; it may last a few days."

Tom, now feeling nervous, shook his head and left the premises.

***

Tom was partially asleep on his couch when he was awakened by the door charm announcing Shelia McGee. Tom said, "Open," as Shelia or "Crystal" entered his room. How was he going to explain to Shelia that she was Crystal? And what was that code that would release the memory blockage, which only his mother knew? A thought came to him: *This lady is a princess from a storybook. The records said that Crystal's personality is very intellectual, but she is hard-nosed and has sarcastic and temperamental traits, which explains Shelia's outburst at Riverside Park yesterday.*

Shelia walked into Tom's room and sat across from him on the sofa with her feet on the coffee table. *She is making herself at home*, Tom thought in amusement.

"Playing lazybones today?" Shelia asked.

Tom smiled and replied, "The center is in lockdown because of a security breach while the Navy is investigating their own."

"Are you a suspect?" Shelia asked with a surprised smile.

Tom wasn't sure if he should laugh or be insulted. "Not too likely, or they would have me interrogated by now."

"Then we should have some free time together," Shelia suggested.

Tom smiled. "We could go hiking, swimming at the beach, or visit some of my friends."

"Sounds like fun. Where do you want to go first?" Tom was surprised by Shelia's determination to start the day.

***

Tom, relaxing on the sandy beach, watched Shelia, who was a short distance away, swimming in the ocean. It had been three days since the center lockdown, and yet, there were no words from his mother. Tom heard a ruffle in the sand beside him and looked up to see his friend Allen, a male nurse, drinking from his beaker, looking ahead.

"Nice girl you got there, Tom."

"Thanks. Is this social or business?" Tom asked.

"Neither. Just a warning," Allen replied. "What's with that skinny kid behind us by the parking lot?"

"You mean the one with the wide-brimmed hat?"

"Ya, that's the one," Allen replied.

"Sharon's replacement, I suppose, since I first saw him at the shopping mall before she left on-call duty."

Allen nodded his head, sorry to hear about Sharon. "She had me fooled, too. Have you heard the latest about the center?"

Tom's eyes perked up, "No, I haven't."

"It's strange. Not a peep about it in the media. Navy Security raided one of their own across town this morning. No names were mentioned, but this guy killed three of the military police while unarmed before he was shot dead. The cleanup crew showed up soon after and emptied the apartment, which is strange, but it means the center should be open soon."

"Thanks, Allen. Anything else?"

Allen sighed, "Yes, there is, and you will not like this news. Your mother is dead."

***

"Why wasn't I told that my mother has been dead for two days!" Tom shouted at the chief editor.

"I'm sorry. We were forced to comply with a gag order, and I thought they would have informed you personally."

"Who authorized the gag order?" Tom demanded.

"I can't say," said the editor. "Look, Tom, the Navy owns and controls this city and planet. You don't mess with their security most of all."

Tom forced himself to be calm and said, "Okay, so it isn't the local authorities but the Navy Security. That's all I need to know." Tom turned on his heels and left the editor's office. He saw that idiot greenhorn still spying on him and was about to confront him when his com-link buzzed.

The com-link voicemail said, "The center lockdown is over. All personnel report to their station."

That was when Tom finally made his decision.

***

Sitting in his center office, Tom inserted his memory disc into the receiver and contemplated his next step.

It's no longer safe to hack into the high-administrator sites; the virus will await me. My father must somehow be involved and is off limits for now. The local authority is likely a dead end, and their coroner would be, too. However, the Navy has its own coroner office.

After Tom had broken into the Navy's coroner site, the mystery got bigger, as there was no listing in his mother's name. Tom searched for an icon that might represent something unusual and found one. He hacked through the seal, and the data on his mother were downloaded.

Tom read the conclusion that it was a possible homicide. An image was available, and Tom held his breath as he opened it. It was not his mother but a naked man. Tom recognized him; he was a cryptologic technician, like himself. *This is very strange. What is going on here? The data fit the description of my mother, but the body is that of a man. The deceased must be the one the police shot and killed this morning. The body certainly looks strong enough to kill anyone with his bare hands if Allen's story is correct. What is this? The coroner had a guest assistant.*

Tom copied the guest assistant's name and some other data and exited the site. He memorized the doctor's name, then noticed that the time was almost up and took the usual protocol of shutting down for the day. When Tom left the center behind, the thought of the doctor's assistant never left his mind.

What is a doctor specializing in alien biological studies doing in the coroner's office? The body in the coroner's office is as human as he is. Is it possible that my mother was murdered? If so, why? This will be a long night for me, Tom thought miserably. *I'm getting in over my head; I need extra help with my investigation.*

Nearly a week later, it was a humid and cloudy day when Tom walked up to a single dwelling and knocked on the door.

"Hi, Andy. Can we gather some best friends together?" This was code for Tom asking for help from the hacker's friends.

"We are pretty busy. What do you have in mind?"

"I have a list of things for the guys to bring along," Tom said as he handed the note to Andy.

After Andy read the note, he asked, "Tom, are you planning on going on holiday?" trying to figure out whether he was leaving town.

"Soon," Tom replied.

Andy sighed, stared at Tom, and slowly shook his head. "I will pass the note over to the guys."

"Thanks, Andy."

***

"Hey, Tom, thanks for the invitation. Aren't you taking a holiday?"

"I am," said Tom.

"Well, next time you're in town, call me, okay?"

Tom shook his head as Buddy was the last to leave his flat. Tom felt weary and started cleaning up when the door charm announced: "Shelia McGee and Manny."

I thought they were looking for a new flat.

"Open," Tom said to the door.

"Hi, Tommy," Shelia said as she and Manny walked in and dropped their bags and packs to the floor.

"What are you guys doing here?" Tom asked.

"We aren't guys, Tommy!"

"It's not Tommy; it's Tom."

"Okay then, we are ladies, not guys, right?" Shelia smiled.

Tom sighed, "What are you ladies doing here?"

"We are looking for a flat in town we like, so we are moving in until we find one because your mother's flat is taken."

"Look, guys, uh ladies, it's not proper for you both to stay over."

"Oh, is it because you are a Christian?"

Tom replied, "That's partly right, but I am leaving town soon."

"Then, could we have your flat?"

"No, it's spoken for already," said Tom.

"Bummer," said Shelia.

"There isn't any place for us tonight, so we are stuck here for the night," said Shelia.

Why does she have to put on that perfect smile? Tom thought. "All right, you can stay the night..."

"Good, as you are the man of the house, will you let Manny and me have your only bedroom?"

Without another word, the ladies carried their possessions into the bedroom. Tom stood about in amazement, having been hoodwinked out of his bedroom.

Manny returned and said, "If you don't mind, I will clean up your flat."

"Be my guest," said Tom. "Manny, please inform Shelia that I will be back in an hour," he said as he put on his jacket and left the flat.

Tom walked to the nearby garden courtyard, feeling secure in being alone. He pulled out his reader and inserted the memory disc that Andy had given him earlier. *Crystal's personality and tomboy background is slowly influencing Shelia's city-girl traits. Not that it matters because Shelia and everything else will be far behind me in a few days,* he thought.

"Good," Tom whispered. *All the guys have their homework. Let's start with Doctor Halley, who assisted the coroner. During the last 60 years, Halley has specialized in two fields: alien biology and mind modification—an odd mixture of medical sciences. This is interesting; he reports only to Rear Admiral Melnyk.*

Doctor Halley had only two assignments in the last two weeks: one was an alien examination, and the other was a mind modification. Someone had likely had their mind wiped clean. Tom couldn't see how the deceased man in the coroner's office was an alien. There was no record of the other person who had their memory wiped clean.

Tom opened the following file and saw his mother, Sheba Steiner. Tom already knew most of the data except for what was in the last data file. His mother had recently become a top security risk! Again, Melnyk was to conduct the interrogation.

Tom opened the following file on Rear Admiral Melnyk. Tom recognized a long list of assignments with no reference to his years in one of the Navy Security branches. Tom scanned the list but didn't recognize any names until he came across one: Captain Mark Styler of the ship *Marvel*, Crystal's father! *Why was Crystal's father investigated?*

Tom opened the following file on Melnyk's right-hand man, who likely did all the dirty work for his father. When he looked up his image, he saw it was Doctor Halley. Tom felt his blood boil. *It's Mother's short-lived boyfriend, Shelton Paterson.* His mother was frightened of Shelton and had told Tom to stay away from him. Tom read his profile, and it was not good. All the details on Shelton's past assignments were sealed tight. Why the double identifications?

Tom opened the final file: a personal message from Andy. It read, "Hello, Tom. I can guess that the reason for requesting this data is for your quest to learn about your mother's disappearance. These files are hot, but we have all learned a lot from you, so we want to return the favor to you. I searched on my own and found something that will greatly interest you. The video was taken shortly after the phony coroner's report.

When you are finished with the video, this disc will erase itself. Good luck, Tom. It was nice knowing you."

Tom opened the video file from a night cam from the parking lot facing toward the medical clinic where Doctor Halley worked as a mind medic. A couple walked out of the clinic door. They walked toward the camera, and their faces were identifiable. Shelton/Doctor Halley and his mother had a blue collar around her neck. A prisoner mind controller. She looked spaced out as it became apparent that her mind had been wiped clean. Then, another disturbing thought hit Tom: *If Halley had downloaded Sheba's memories, they would know about Shelia/Crystal and Manny!*

Chapter 5

Several weeks later, inside a dim room, two clinical personnel in white medical uniforms stood over a patient lying on a bed.

"Doctor Halley, the process is nearly complete," said the nurse. "The patient is responding normally and is now receiving the modified memory."

Doctor Halley looked up from the reader in his hand. "Good, you may call it a day, Nurse."

"Thank you, Doctor Halley," the nurse said as she left the room.

The doctor walked nearby to the wall console, checked the terminal, and then the patient. Satisfied, he called the nursing station. "You can bring in Admiral Melnyk," he said.

The admiral joined Halley as he walked into the room. The admiral looked down on the patient and asked, "Did he respond to the mind wipe successfully?"

"According to the computer's analysis, it is complete."

"Can he hear us?" Melnyk asked.

"No. He will be out for a little while longer."

The admiral nodded his head. "Tom, you are a very foolish young man like your mother. You should have kept your nose out of Navy Security affairs." Melnyk asked Halley, "What about that girl and the android?"

"The android has been reprogrammed and shipped off-world. As for the girl, I placed a permanent blockage on her memory. Any updated news about her uncle and family?" asked the doctor.

Melnyk replied, "It's almost certain they met their demise in warp space."

"Which also means so did Doctor McGee," the doctor sighed.

"You knew the doctor before, didn't you?" Melnyk asked.

"I have known Doctor McGee since our school years. We shared the same medical background in physiology sensory memory, and both specialized in cognitive neuroscience memory."

"It's too bad Sheba came across the *Marvel* report; none of this mind wipe business would have been necessary."

"Are you finished with the cyborg?" Melnyk asked.

Halley replied, "My report is almost complete, but there is nothing new to add for the record."

"Another mind meltdown?" the admiral muttered as he remembered how the cyborg had killed his three agents.

"Unfortunately, yes," the doctor replied. "The cyborg's body was cremated this morning."

"For our sake, it's important that the inner circle upstairs doesn't know about Tom and Sheba. The cyborg report, of course, will be forwarded to them."

"Do you think your sponsorship for the committee inner circle will be realized someday?" Halley asked.

"Yes, as long they don't know about our mistake, we will be fine," Melnyk replied. "I am finished here; my men will be here later tonight to take them both away. I will see you tomorrow morning in my office with your report. Goodnight, Doctor."

When Tom was left alone, the blue cap on his head shifted to red. Tom's eyes opened, and he quietly raised himself from the bed, walked to the control panel, and searched the data. Tom eventually found what he was looking for and downloaded the data to his memory disc. He removed the disc, walked back, and lay back down on the bed. The head cap's red color shifted back to blue, and the room again became quiet.

***

"This isn't exactly one of your better plans," Shelia said dryly. "'Trust me', you said, and look where we are now. On a stupid prison boat."

"It's a ship, not a boat."

"Who cares what it's called! You said we were going to an outpost planet. Instead, we are going to an exiled group of convicts!" Shelia cried.

"They are mostly political exiles," Tom said defiantly.

"Tom, if I could, I would have beaten you to a pulp. I still don't know who I am, Shelia or Crystal."

"There is no question you are Crystal," said Tom.

"I know that, but my memory is permanently locked," Shelia shouted.

"If we can find a specialist to remove the new lock, I can give you the code to remove your blockage."

"I suppose you should get the credit for that," Shelia smiled. "It was clever of you to set yourself up for a false mind wipe. You were lucky your friend Allen works at the mind clinic and overrode the control center. Did you download all of your mother's stolen memories?"

"Yes, which is how I found your code when Manny forwarded Jayson's messages to my mother."

Shelia sat beside Tom, "I should thank you for the trouble you went through in helping get my memory back. What do you think will happen when we arrive at this place?"

"It's in Sector Two, not far from the new Sector Five, about a two-week trip. If I had more time at the Academy, I could have given you a better answer. All I know is that there is a structured system to maintain order in their society. They don't have correctional officers per se, but there is a former police system set up to keep everyone in line. Something like the Australian open penal colony system back on Old Earth during the 1800s. There is some semi-freedom. Hopefully, we can plan our next step."

"What is our next step?" Shelia asked.

"Find out how we can fit into their society and find my mother."

"You don't know for sure if she is there?"

"That's true. But if we find my mother, things will start to look up for us," Tom smiled.

Crystal snuggled up to Tom and said, "You better hope you have a good plan. Otherwise, I will beat you to a pulp!"

Tom grinned, "I will try to remember that."

***

"Shelia McGee, please come to desk number four." Shelia walked over to the desk and sat across from a petite woman in a plain black government uniform.

"I am Kristy." Without looking at her reader, she asked, "Why are you here?"

"Too many ornery people back home wanted me off-world," Shelia smiled.

"If you are going to be sarcastic with me, I have just the place for you," Kristy said in a firm voice.

"All I can tell you is what I can remember. My father is a private doctor for King Stevenson. I was shot and woke up to find myself in Planet Academy orbit. And then I was shipped here."

"Your report does say that your father is a doctor. You haven't finished your nursing degree, but there is a spot for you as a nursing aid. I will download the data for your employment and living quarters to your implant. You may leave."

"I have a friend," Shelia said. "His name is Tom Beegle; we want to stay together."

Kristy read Tom Beegle's profile records. "A political advocate, a drifter, and a recluse, too. All the employment he is meant for is labor."

"Tom is brilliant; he knows much about computer networks and system analysis."

"I don't have that on his record," said Lisa.

"Tom taught himself everything he knows."

Kristy frowned and said, "I could place him on labor in the same zone and let the administrators decide what else they can do with him. Bring Tom here, and we will go from there."

***

Tom was wheeling a cart down a hallway full of medical supplies and stopped when he heard a familiar voice call out his name. Shelia walked out from behind the nursing station. "Sorry about your job; it's the best I could do for you."

"I don't mind it at all; it's a nice change from sitting behind the desk. What about you and your nursing job?"

63

"The clinic is short on staff, not just here, but most other places. That's why I am doing more as a nurse than as a nurse aide. There is also a shortage of flats, but I have been given a room in barrack number 3."

"The Same for me. My barracks are just next door to yours. Will I meet you in the mess hall?" Tom asked.

Shelia replied, "For sure. See you later."

Tom waited for Shelia at the entrance door before entering. "It's a huge hall; there must be 500 seats here," Tom said in astonishment. The hall was filled with 500 men and women, making it harder for them to hear each other.

"Let's get in the lineup; the smorgasbord of food choices is not bad," Shelia said. After Tom and Shelia filled their plate, they walked along the row of tables until they found an empty spot for two.

"Keep walking, buddy; those two seats are mine," a booming voice said behind them. Tom turned and faced the most significant guy he had ever seen.

"Never mind, Tom. Two guys over at the next table just left their seats," Shelia suggested.

"Smart lady. Don't forget to take your baby brother with you," the man smirked.

Bothered by the man's stinging remark, Tom took his seat beside Shelia. "Just for the record, how come you never stood up to that guy like you did back at the River Park on Academy?"

"Tom, I don't even know why I did that in the first place. You know more about Crystal than I do, which seems so strange."

"When we are alone, I will give you a more detailed profile of Crystal. Crystal seems to be like nobody else I have ever known. I can tell you one thing, Shelia: Even with the memory blockage, you are slowly taking on Crystal's personality. Have you got the weekend off starting tomorrow?"

"Yes. How about you, Tom?"

With his mouth full, Tom nodded his head.

An overhead buzzer alarm startled Shelia, "What is that all about?"

"It's all right," said the man across the table. "It's only an alarm test."

"For what?" Shelia asked.

"You must be new here. Even though this planet looks peaceful, it's not. The weather can be quite violent, with sudden hurricane-strength downdraft winds from the coastal mountain range nearby. You will notice that the trees are quite short with extremely thick stems. All the buildings here are no more than a single story tall," the man smiled. "My name is Jones, by the way," he said as he shook hands with Tom and Shelia.

"Tom Beegle and Shelia McGee," said Tom. "What do you do here, Jones?" Tom asked.

"I'm a sub-administrator for the town network. I help coordinate the town's finances and programmers."

"Tom is good with computer analysis," Shelia said.

"If we ever need one in the future, that's good to know. Why are you two here?" Jones asked.

"It's hard to say; we have a memory block," Shelia replied.

"That is surprising. Most newcomers get to keep their memory nowadays. Too many sloppy mind manipulations only created more problems, usually depression. You probably know by now that most of us are political exiles or troublemakers."

"How do the authorities keep everything in order?" Tom asked.

"You could be assigned a good or dirty job," Jones smiled. "Otherwise, you get hungry very quickly."

"What about outsiders?" Tom inquired.

"Highly restricted, as most ships cannot go beyond the orbit station, and the few require the blue-collar. No exceptions."

"Who is the warden?" said Tom.

"My wife," Jones laughed as he stood up to leave. "I will see you again someday."

Tom and Shelia watched as Jones walked out of the mess hall. "Is he kidding us?" Shelia asked.

"If he is, it's a good joke! Can I see you after work?" Tom asked.

Shelia paused for a second. "All right," she said as she quickly rose from her chair and left Tom behind.

What was that all about? Tom wondered.

Later that day, Tom sat on the bench outside the clinic, waiting for Shelia.

"Okay, let's go," Shelia said as she walked past Tom. Tom looked up in surprise and rushed to catch up with Shelia.

"Where are we going?" Tom asked. Shelia didn't reply but kept walking. "Shelia, do you mind if I ask you a question?" Tom changed the question.

"What?" she snarled as she turned around to face Tom.

"Why are you upset?"

"Tom, don't you understand? I can't reason with myself. You have to spend a day in my head to understand me. I know I am not Shelia, yet I have her memory. My real self is locked away, perhaps forever, and I may never get it back. I feel like two people trapped in one body. Tom, which one of us do you prefer? Is it Shelia or Crystal?"

"It could be both, and that may be a royal plus," Tom smiled.

"This isn't a joke, Tom!" Shelia shouted with a harsh stare.

"You are right; that was a stupid remark. Let's find a place along this walkway to talk alone, and I will tell you everything I know about Crystal. We've got two hours before nightfall, and I was told it gets windy. Would that bench over there do okay?" Tom pointed.

"It is as good as any," said Shelia, taking his arm.

***

Tom was sweeping the clinic's hallway floor when one of the nurses approached him.

"Mister Beegle, the Boss wants to see you in her office. Don't worry about the Boss; she seems in a good mood today."

Tom had to learn quickly; the clinic manager preferred to be known as the 'Boss'. When Tom tried to find out her formal name, she angrily exploded. From then on, Tom tried his best to stay out of her way. Like everything else, basic technology was the norm as Tom knocked on the Boss' door.

"Come on in," the Boss said. She was smiling as she asked Tom to sit down. *This doesn't seem right*, thought Tom. "You asked to see me, Boss?"

"I did. We have a special guest today. You have been here two months now, and I didn't know you knew the warden."

Tom took a hint and decided to play the game. "Is Jones coming, too?" Tom asked.

"You mean her husband? I haven't been told."

So, Jones wasn't kidding after all.

"The warden has made a personal request to meet with you later today. You may take the rest of the day off, with pay, of course," the Boss smiled.

"I do appreciate your generosity. It's been a good two months of employment, Boss." *It must have taken much effort to smile like that*, Tom thought.

The Boss, relieved and trying to excuse herself, said, "You may go now; the warden should be here anytime now."

Tom stood up to leave, thought for a second, and asked, "Would you mind if Shelia came with me?"

The Boss stopped herself from appearing annoyed, "Shelia is a friend of yours, isn't she? Very well, you can tell her yourself. She is welcome to join you if she wishes."

"Thank you, Boss," Tom said as he left the office. He walked to the nursing station and saw Shelia finishing with a patient.

"Hi, Shelia. I've got some good news. The warden wants to see me, and you get to come with me, with pay."

"What does the warden want with you?"

"I don't know yet, but we should get a change of clothes. The warden will be here soon to pick us up. I'll meet you in the main lobby in a few minutes." Tom stopped momentarily, then continued, "Bring a change of clothes, too." Without hesitation, Tom kissed Shelia and turned on his heel toward the men's changing room.

"Tom!" Shelia shouted as she walked up to him. She whispered near Tom's face, "That's the first time you've ever kissed me."

Tom felt a little awkward and asked, "Are you upset?"

"I should clobber you for the kiss, but I'll leave it for another day," she said as she walked by Tom with a smile.

Tom decided to put on his old clothes and ensured all his concealed pouches were in place. He walked to the main lobby and sat on a couch. Shelia sat beside Tom and said, "Who is this Warden?"

"I am completely in the dark, just as you are. The Boss is shaken up about it, and she's scared out of her wits," Tom smiled.

"Something is coming; it looks like a flitter[1]. It's a new model Turbo 8 P, eight-seater, Commonwealth Executive flitter," remarked Shelia. "King Stevenson had a similar one."

"Have you been in one of those flitters?" Tom asked.

"From Shelia's memory, a few times, but Crystal used it a lot with her grandfather," Shelia sighed.

"You mean to say that Crystal flew the flitter herself?" Tom asked.

---

[1] A Frigate, Lightweight land craft, Interplanetary, Transfer personal Transport, Emergency anchorage and Reconnaissance vehicle.

Shelia nodded.

The flitter landed at the reserved spot near the parking lot. A man in blackjack boots stepped out of the flitter, walked toward the clinic door, and stood before Tom. "Mr. Beegle," the man in black said in more of a statement than a question.

Tom replied, "I am, and my friend Shelia is coming with me." The man in black looked at Shelia, smiled, and said, "Very well. She may come, too. Follow me, please," as he led them to the flitter.

Tom, surprised by the luxurious, spacious interior of the flitter, sat near the front row with Shelia.

"Mr. Beegle, the warden is still preoccupied at her office, so that she will join us later. In the meantime, we will wait for her at the warden's private retreat several thousand kilometers north. I'll turn on the viewer. Enjoy the view."

"We are already in the air!" Tom said in amazement.

"The anti-gravity plates on the floor cancel out the sensation of movement," the man smiled.

"Thank you. Whoever you are."

"I am the warden's butler. Just call me 'Mr. Bob'," he said as he left the room to join the pilot beyond the cabin door.

"Any idea who this warden is?" Shelia asked.

Tom shook his head and said, "When we find out, I'm sure it will be a surprise."

"According to the wall clock timer, we have 20 minutes before we arrive at the retreat," said Shelia as she rested her head on Tom's shoulder and closed her eyes. "Wake me up before we arrive."

When the flitter's clock charm woke up Shelia, she looked at the viewer and saw a peach-colored Victorian-style manor surrounded by a large open lawn several hundred acres in size. The resort was a large horseshoe shape and inside a 500-hundred-foot-high crater was facing the ocean.

"It looks like the retreat is protected from hurricane-force winds from the coastal mountain range," Tom remarked.

"How can the warden afford this retreat?" Shelia asked.

"That is easy to answer," Mr. Bob replied. "Fifty years ago, it was owned by a wealthy industrious elite. There was a fallout between the elite and the previous warden. The warden had him arrested and seized the resort. The estate was put up for sale, but there were no takers. The warden made the estate a permanent retreat for the Commonwealth-appointed warden."

The flitter landed on the pad near the estate. As Tom, Shelia, and Mr. Bob exited the flitter, the craft returned for the warden. The butler showed Tom and Shelia their bedrooms. Tom was overwhelmed by the luxury and size of the estate, but Shelia felt right at home.

"Mr. Bob, could you please give us a tour of the estate?"

As Mr. Bob showed Tom and Shelia the estate, he said, "There are fifteen bedrooms, a kitchen, a living room, two dens, an exercise room, and a pool. The retreat is operated by four staff members, one chef, two maids, and me."

"The warden has just arrived, and she would like to meet in the den if you would please." Tom and Shelia followed the butler to the den, and they sat on one of the four sofas near the gas fireplace.

Moments later, they heard the door open, and a familiar voice said, "Welcome, Tom Beegle, or should I say, Tom

Steiner?" Tom and Shelia stood up and turned toward the speaker. They looked shocked when they recognized the unknown warden.

"Sharon?" Tom said.

Chapter 6

"Off-warp jump countdown will begin in 5, 4, 3, 2, 1. Our destination is on target," the pilot announced.

"That's the longest four weeks I've ever spent in Warp Space. Jennifer was beginning to get old-fashioned cabin fever," said Jayson.

The captain laughed, "So too were our spouses, Jayson."

"We have contact with Midway Station," said the pilot.

Midway Station, a solid 3034-mile-wide iron asteroid, was operated by a private consolidated group of former politicians and retired CEOs. The midway point was located between Commonwealth Sector 2 and Territorial Sector 5. Midway acted as a refueling station, hotel, trading post, and hiding place.

"Put them on an open channel," the captain ordered.

"This is Midway Station; your ship is not identifiable."

"I am sorry. This is Captain Ted Fredrickson; our ship ID has been disabled. Please advise."

"Maintain a stationary orbit and prepare for inspection."

"Captain, may I cut in?" said Jayson.

"Be my guest."

"Midway Station, we request communication contact with Chief Inspector Lisa, code word 'thunderbolt'."

"Acknowledged. Please stand by."

"What is the code thunderbolt?" the Captain asked.

"I mentioned two code words: Chief Inspector Lisa, which refers to their boss, and thunderbolt identified me."

"Who is their boss?"

"This is Midway; the inspection is canceled, and our probe will meet up with you shortly. The probe will lead your ship to one of our underground docking stations. Please maintain radio silence."

A short time later, a blue-flashing probe met up with the yacht and returned to the asteroid.

"All right," the captain said to the pilot, "follow the probe." The yacht followed the blue probe down to the surface, well away from the main ship's surface docking station. The probe descended deep into a large depression and then entered an opening in a wall door. The yacht slowly entered as the door closed behind them.

"Captain, I suggest that the crew and their family stay behind until we receive authorization to step off the ship."

"Agreed. Do we have the leverage to negotiate?"

"Come and see," Jayson smiled.

Captain Ted and Jayson arrived at the docking tube to the main lobby when a voice cried out, "Jayson!" A sandy-blond-haired woman embraced Jayson and then stepped back. "It's been so long. Are Jennifer and the girls here, too?" the woman asked.

"Just Jennifer and my youngest daughter, Jenny. May I introduce you to Captain Ted Frederickson?"

"Captain, this is Samantha Stevenson, Midway's chairman of the board, and also my grandmother," Jayson smiled.

***

"Both of you must have a lot on your mind," said Samantha as she leaned back in her chair. "I assumed the last four weeks had given you and your people some ideas regarding your plans?"

"Yes, they have, but we would appreciate any valuable input from you," Jayson suggested.

"There are some propositions: one would be to reregister your ship. It may not fool the Commonwealth Authority in the four sectors, but you will be safe in the fifth territorial sector. The Commonwealth is a long way from setting up a traffic control center. We could change your identification and send you on your way to several different forerunner planets nearby."

"Or you could take part in our grand project here on Midway. Let me show you what I mean by that." Samantha stood up and waved her hand at a 6 by 12-foot blackened glass window behind her. The window revealed an incredible sight—a huge underground cavern world. Jayson looked beyond at a slight concave in the distance where the surface was one huge park-like environment. There were small lakes with sailing boats and trees of every sort from different worlds as well as birds and small animals. Two continual lines of lights stretched along the ceiling. Public transport of various types discreetly merged within the environment. All along the side walls near the surface were many story-high rolls of windows and door entrances where the inhabitants lived.

The captain stood near the window and said to Jayson, "This is fascinating. Did you know about this?"

Jayson replied, "I'd heard of it, but I didn't know it was this massive."

Samantha broke in, "What you gentlemen are witnessing is only the beginning stage. About 10 to 20 miles below ground is a ring of tunnels and caves that link or partly link together and circle Midway. This cave is 10 to 15 miles wide, 40 miles long, and three to five miles high. All the building materials were found not far from Midway: frozen water, minerals, methane, nitrogen, and asteroids were in abundance."

"The next cave in line is planned to be made into an industrial complex, and we are now asking for help to kick start stage two. Midway was discovered 50 years ago by a Commonwealth explorer. After my husband died 40 years ago, because of my royal political connections and expertise, I was asked if I would like to take on a project to transform a dead world into a living habitat. During the last ten years, we have transplanted the best of ten world creatures. We could use your help, gentlemen."

***

Jayson and Jennifer sat together at the kitchen table and watched Samantha play with her great-grandchild, Jenny, on the living room floor.

"We could make a good life here, Jayson. Jenny would be safe here in this habitat, and we could be, too. But you're not happy about settling down here, are you?"

"It's not that; there's something missing here. I don't think we are getting a full picture of this place. If this habitat is so wonderful, why is the population so low? There should have been tens of thousands of people in the habitat by now. And the air has a metallic, iron taste; I am not sure we could get used to it."

Samantha paused and said, "You are right about the population and the air. One option is to build a series of metal air purifier towers that could ionize any airborne smog particles. The clean air could be expelled through vents in the lower part of the tower."

"The other option is a slight modification of the inhabitants' genes that would fix the sensation of the metallic taste. However, any genetic changes will bring the wrath of the Commonwealth authorities down on our heads. They will not hesitate to shut down our medical lab and even perform a mind wipe on the doctors without a trial."

"But why? That's so drastic," Jennifer cried.

Samantha shook her head in agreement, "During my eighty years, I have yet to understand their laws and actions regarding genetic modifications. The law is strict and is not open to debate."

"What about the habitat's population," Jayson asked.

"The turnaround is quite high. Besides the air problem, some rumors have spread around that the Navy wants to take over Midway. It does make sense for the Navy to seize Midway for security and to use it as a jumping point when Sector Five is officially established."

Samantha paused, then added, "My opinion is that neither of these is true, though. When the Commonwealth cut back on the grants, I knew something else was going on. My only clue is that all ten major Navy bases just the other week canceled on-duty personnel leaves. All off-duty personnel and reserves are required to be ready to report for duty on short notice. But my sources could not find any credible threat to the Commonwealth."

"What about the Thracian?" Jayson asked.

Samantha replied, "During the Imperial era, fifty-five years ago, we were at war against the small Thracian Empire, an alien warlord society. This was a ten-year war the Empire narrowly won. Soon afterward, the Empire formed a new alliance and renamed it the Commonwealth. I have considered the Thracian as a threat, but there are no records of any hostile aggression toward the Commonwealth. But there are some reports of missing ships near the borderlands."

Jayson recalled the treaty that was signed between the two factions involving a circular area, fifty light-years across by five light-years deep; this was an unmanned border referred to as the Borderland.

"I know what you are thinking, Jayson; New Sweoland is not far from the Borderland. We can only hope that our family and friends took your advice to leave home to avoid prosecution from the present government."

Jayson muttered, "Some are too stubborn to listen, which is why I sent Crystal away by force."

"I wonder how Crystal is doing now?" said Jennifer. "Crystal should have come under Sheba Steiner's care three weeks ago."

"Not to worry. I am certain that Crystal is in God's hands," said Jayson.

Three weeks later

Solar System Academy, Planet Academy – The Commonwealth Navy War Room

A large 3D hologram image appeared above a low platform in the middle of the dimly lit room. The hologram was surrounded by eleven chairs representing the ten admirals of the ten major Commonwealth navies throughout the Four Sectors. Rear Admiral Melnyk entered the room, and the holographic focus showed a solar system of nonlinear planetary formations.

"You may begin, Rear Admiral Melnyk," said the chairman.

"Thank you, Mr. Chairman. The Navy Security has made an amazing effort in locating the Robotic, now referred to as the 'Bots', and their secret home base just inside the Borderland. In the past several years, we have installed over a dozen hidden spy cams just outside the solar system and beyond. We are confident that none of our spy cams have been discovered."

One of the admirals cut in, "It has been over 100 years since we won our war with the Bots and since their ringleader escaped into unknown space. How can we be sure another Bot home base doesn't exist?"

"We can't be sure, but it is reasonable to assume, based on observations, that there is no usual traffic outside the Borderland."

"Please continue," the chairman requested.

"The bulk of the Bots' activity lies in this world," Melnyk pointed, "a non-atmosphere minor planet. All of which is hidden underground of course."

"What about their cyborgs," one of the admirals asked.

"Yes, their cyborgs today are different from the original cyborgs, which were half machine and half human. Today, cyborgs are built by 4D printers using synthetic human DNA. Their minds are still constructed from crystal gel and have a robotic-like configuration. One major difference is their double layer of muscle fiber, which gives them a huge increase in strength. This would be an extremely rare occurrence among homo sapiens. The cyborgs are living among us. Fortunately, we know who they are, and our security is keeping a close watch on them."

"But not all of them," one of the admirals insisted.

"True," Melnyk replied. "As for the Bots' home-world, we know that one day they will become a major threat to us all."

"Not to mention the Thracian Empire," another admiral said in disgust.

"It was demonstrated that the Thracian would someday re-establish their warlord alliance and plan their next expansion, which is why I asked you all here tonight. Our operational nightmare has already started, but we did not begin it."

The admirals rumbled as they stood up straight. Some looked worried and shocked, while others looked angry.

"Explain, Melnyk," the chairman said.

"Yes, sir. Our early spy cams planted throughout the Thracian Sector have recorded enormous efforts in new battleship construction. We severely underestimated the Thracian warlords' ship-building capabilities."

"How did you learn about this?" the chairman asked.

"Mr. Chairman, as you know, Operation Nightmare's strategy was to prepare an attack ship design in the robot configuration and deliver a single major hit to their major economic headquarters. Like the Bots, the ship is fully operated by the ship computer, which fired on their its designated target and then retreats as planned. The Thracian honor system would be their downfall, as it required an immediate response before they could analyze who the attackers were. The Thracian scout ships would soon discover the Bots' base. Our latest spy cam is part of the new experimental Warp Net Communication, which has been built into the system. We can now watch live the war actions." All the Commonwealth battleships were on standby, waiting for orders to proceed and destroy any surviving ship and then continue to the Thracian Empire.

"Observe," Melnyk said, as he pointed to the hologram beside him. New images appeared, showing a massive number of ships surrounding the bots' home base solar system. All ten admirals and the chairman rose to their feet.

"This can't be," one admiral shouted.

"We haven't a hope in prayer," another admiral cried. Several admirals walked around the hologram to study the images.

"Computer, analyze the image statistics," the chairman demanded.

"Eighty-nine destroyers, sixty frigates, ten carriers, 15,000 fighter flitters," the computer replied.

"We are outnumbered four to one," the chairman muttered.

"Look, something else is going on at the Bots' base," someone shouted.

No words could describe the site of the thousands of Bot ships. The design had never been seen before, and they were incredibly fast and extremely deadly. Despite the Thracians' having vastly superior firepower, the Bots' ships were able to maneuver much quicker than the Thracian fighter ships, and it wasn't long before the Thracian fighters were destroyed.

Then, the Bots moved in on the destroyers. The destroyers threw everything they had at them: pulse cannons, lasers, missiles, neutron beams, but the Bots kept on coming. When the Bots were close enough, their weapons sliced through the protective shield. First, the carriers, then the destroyers, and the frigates were destroyed one by one.

In a last desperate move, four of the destroyers broke through and aimed for the Bots' home base. The four destroyers' weapons blasted the minor planet in an attempt to destroy the underground base. In the end, it was a complete holocaust on both sides. Neither side escaped destruction.

The war room was in complete silence until someone said, "I don't understand, the Thracian knew they were losing the battle. Why didn't they retreat to save their own?"

Melnyk responded, "It's part of their two-thousand-year war culture; for them to admit failure is to bring dishonor and shame to their family. The Thracian would rather commit suicide than face the clans in defeat."

"Gentlemen, I recommend we immediately follow through on operation 'Nightmare'," the chairman suggested. A quick agreement was reached among the ten admirals. One by one, the admirals left the war room until the chairman and Melnyk were left alone.

"Whoever came up with the name 'Nightmare' must be a prophet," said Melnyk.

The chairman grunted and said, "I want your best security men to gather anything of value on the Bots' home base. Take extra consideration that no one knows the truth about the Bots." The chairman moved his face inches away from Melnyk's face, "And no security leaks!"

"Yes, sir," said Melnyk.

Chapter 7
Prison Planet

Shelia stepped off of the pool ladder, picked up the towel from the nearby rack, dried herself, and sat down next to Tom.

"You look bored. Still trying to decide who's better looking, Sharon or me?"

Tom, lost in thought, realized that Shelia was talking to him. "Sorry, I didn't mean to ignore you, but you are right, I am bored. It's been three weeks, and I think we've overstayed our welcome here."

"Sharon doesn't seem to think so," Shelia smiled.

Tom, feeling a little awkward, whispered, "Sharon is married, and her husband might hear you."

"It's okay. Sharon and I had a frank conversation the other night."

Tom now gave her his undivided attention.

"To begin with, Sharon and her husband are former spies for the Commonwealth Security."

"We both knew that," said Tom.

"Hush, I am still talking! Sharon cares about you. You're the only one assigned to her that respects her as a friend. Sharon likes you and your mother's honest devotion as Christians; it's not a false front like many of the others she had doubts about in the past."

"Ready for this one," Shelia grinned. "Sharon knows you are a top-grade computer hacker." Tom looked at Shelia in alarm. "Don't worry, Sharon never told anyone. She is very good at her job."

"No kidding," Tom remarked, feeling relieved.

"Sharon's real age is over 60, but her appearance is far less than 35 years of age."

"How did she accomplish looking no older than 35?" Tom asked.

"Sharon was told by the superiors early in her career that if she was going to be effective in her job as some innocent, young, naive girl, she needed to take a daily injection to keep her appearance at 25."

"If she is so good at her job, why did she quit and take on the warden position?" Tom asked.

"I asked Sharon the same question. The side effects of the injections finally caught up with her. When she rolled up her sleeve, the injection site on her upper arm looked like plastic."

"That must have scared her," Tom said.

Shelia nodded her head and said, "When Sharon realized she needed to get off the youth injections, her career was over. In time, her appearance will age until she appears between 35 and 40. Sharon still has another 60 years to go before the threshold; then, her body will break down."

"As for the warden position, there are two reasons for her taking on the job. Sharon has a degree in psychology and criminology. And the other...you are not going to like this one. There is another war coming, and she doesn't want to be a part of it."

"What war?" Tom asked.

"Sharon doesn't know, but she thinks it has to do with the Thracian Empire again. If it is the Thracian, we are a long way from the Borderland, so we should be safe. She told me one more thing," she said as she sat on Tom's knee. "Sharon thinks you are in love with me. How come you never told me this?"

Tom replied, "It's something my mother kept drilling into me; I shouldn't tell women my feelings until three months have gone by."

Shelia leaned toward Tom's face and said, "It's three months now. Is there something you would like to tell me?"

"Sorry to interrupt, but Sharon is due any minute and has made a formal request for you both to wait for her in the den."

Shelia dropped her head on Tom's chest and said in a dry voice, "THANK YOU, MR. BOB." She then rose to her feet and walked back to her room.

***

Sharon walked into the den and sat in her chair across from Tom and Shelia.

"You look tired," said Shelia.

"I am exhausted. I have some bad news. The Commonwealth is officially at war with the Thracian Empire and Shelia, or I should say, Crystal, your home-world, New Sweoland, is caught in the crossfire. If you are thinking about going home and helping your people, I wouldn't recommend it. The government has blamed the royal family for the lack of protection and defense. You will be arrested and perhaps held in prison for life."

"Is there something else?" Tom asked.

"Yes, because we are now officially at war, martial law is in force. That means every major administration will have a security overlord. When the overlord is assigned to me, I will not be able to explain your presence. You will have to leave this place tonight. There is no point in sending you back to the dormitory, as the overlord will question the discrepancy on your records. There is no choice; I am arranging for you both to be sent off-world. There is only one ship leaving tonight, and Mr. Bob will make sure there will be no questions asked."

"Where is the ship heading?"

"Midway," Sharon replied.

***

"This cargo ship is a rust bucket," Shelia said to Tom. I am not impressed with this mess hall either. Everything about this ship is so dilapidated. They have converted a small part of the cargo hold for the women's section."

"They did the same for the men in the other cargo area," said Tom.

"I didn't think the Commonwealth would allow this ship to pass inspection," said Shelia.

"Rules are made to be broken way out in the frontier sector," Tom grinned. "At least it is only a four-day warp jump. When this ship arrives at Midway, we will get off and sign up for a one-year contract. I hope Sharon is right that we aren't stepping into another hellhole; there's something about a restoration project. It's too bad Sharon had an emergency call from her office; we would have learned more about this project."

A thump on the table across from them interrupted the conversation. "Well, look who is here, the little lady and her baby brother," the giant laughed.

Tom groaned. "It's that enormous guy, Bert, again."

"I suppose you are looking for work on Midway?" Shelia asked.

86

"Maybe, maybe not," Bert replied with his mouth full.

"What skills do you have?" Shelia asked.

"The sort of skill I have is beating up people," Bert grinned. "When I am smiling, that should be enough to scare you. I thought I wanted a career; it turns out, I just wanted a credit on my account."

"I think what Bert is saying is that he wants to be a security guard," Shelia said to Tom.

Bert nodded his head and said to Shelia, "You are quick. But I don't do much of that anymore, just mostly labor. Being a guard, I find most men are annoying, but then, some end up dead," Bert laughed.

Tom watched Bert finish with his meal and crush his cup in his huge hand. Tom was shocked by Bert's strength. *If he decides to turn on me, I'm dead.*

"Watch your back. Some of the guys here are a bad bunch. The crew included. I'm on hold #4 if you need me. If you want, I will keep an eye on your baby brother," Bert said to Shelia.

Shelia looked at Tom's red face, "Bert, I would appreciate it if you called my man 'Tom.'"

Bert sighed, "All right, 'Tom' it is. See you guys later." He rose from his chair and wandered off.

"Aren't you going to thank me?" Shelia asked.

"Do you mean that?" Tom asked.

"Mean what?" Sharon replied.

"That I am your man?"

"If we were alone, I could tell you a lot more," Shelia whispered in Tom's ear. "Let's walk around this ship; maybe we can find something interesting. Everything inside this ship is basic. Of course, now I understand why Mr. Bob bypassed the security check-in and got us onboard in the middle of the night. We couldn't see the outside of the ship. It's an old Imperial Navy merchant marine cargo ship, but the main cargo area is partitioned into many smaller holds. That's why the ship is the metallic gray gun steel. When the Commonwealth took over, the Navy gradually phased out the gun steel and replaced it with more modern gray synthetic steel."

"That's as far as you go, guys. Turn around and go back where you came from," the security guard said with a threatening gesture.

"Sorry, we didn't know this place is out of bounds," said Tom.

A loud voice yelled behind the security man, "I don't care how or why it happens, get that pathetic computer fixed, Captain."

A man stormed off in a huff and walked out of sight, and the captain looked dismayed. The captain turned back toward the bridge entrance when Shelia yelled, "Captain! My friend is a computer analyst; maybe he could help you."

The captain looked doubtful, "I don't know, it is obsolete, long before your time, son."

"You should let Tom try, sir. He is very good at it," Shelia pled.

"Okay, come with me," said the captain.

"No, you don't, lady. Just your friend," the guard said.

Tom turned to the captain and concocted a story: "Sir, Shelia is my assistant. She is a pilot and navigator."

"So young, too. All right, you both can come."

They entered the bridge, which was an eye-opener for Tom. The captain was right, as not just the computer, but everything was obsolete. All the console covers were open, revealing their internal components. The technicians were working to fix the problems.

"What did you find," the captain demanded.

"Another short. I bypassed the system, but the computer is still down."

The captain said to Tom, "All right, this is your department."

Tom sat at the computer console, accessed his implant, and downloaded the old Imperial computer program and systematic layout. Once Tom understood the system, he started working.

An hour later, Tom said to the captain, "I'm finished. Please inform your pilot; I am ready to test the system."

"I can't, as the pilot is in sickbay as well as the reserve pilot," the captain said dryly.

"What has happened to the pilots?" Shelia asked.

"They were found overdosed together in their room," the captain replied.

Tom interrupted, "Sir, I don't think they are addicts; your crewmen may have been drugged. Your ship's computer was hacked by an incompetent programmer. Someone inserted a program to drop the ship out of warp space. Instead, the program caused a shortage in the system. If I hadn't fixed and reinstalled the program, we would never have dropped out of warp space. I guess that a pirate would be waiting for us when we are in normal space. But my recommendation is to make sure the system is working okay. And we need a qualified pilot."

"Never mind, I will do it," Shelia said as she sat in the pilot's chair.

The captain and Tom stood by and watched in astonishment as Shelia performed the start-up protocol by synchronizing with the ship's computer. When Shelia was finished, she said, "Ship Computer, navigation report."

"All systems online," replied the computer.

"I will get extra security and inform my boss," said the captain.

When Tom and Shelia were alone, he said, "Was that you or Crystal that had the pilot expertise?"

"I don't recall Shelia having the pilot knowledge, so it must be Crystal." Shelia rose from her chair and wrapped her arms around Tom's neck. In a soft, quiet voice, Shelia asked, "Who are you in love with, Shelia or Crystal?"

Just then a crew member entered the bridge. Shelia, upset, released herself from Tom and stormed off the bridge.

Tom whispered, "I don't know, Shelia, or is it Crystal?"

***

"We should come here a few minutes earlier next time to beat the lineup for a meal; I don't seem to have much patience for this lately."

"Excuse me, are you Tom Beegle and Shelia McGee?"

They turned to face one of the ship's crew members.

"Yes, we are. Who's asking?" Shelia replied.

"The captain requested you to both join him for dinner in his quarters."

Tom and Shelia looked at each other. "Yes, we would love to," said Shelia.

"Good, if you will follow me."

A voice called out from behind a short distance, "Hey guys, how's it going?"

"Hi, Bert. We are going to have dinner with the captain," said Shelia. "We will get together another time, okay?"

Feeling a little hurt, Bert said, "No problem, have a good time, you guys." He watched them being led off to the captain's quarters. Then, a scowl replaced Bert's smile.

"This is the captain's quarters. I will leave you here. Just knock on the door and enter."

Tom looked at Shelia, shrugged his shoulders, and knocked on the door. Tom and Shelia entered the room and saw a powerfully built crewman choking the captain with one hand, holding him up against the wall. The crewman caught off guard, dropped the unconscious man to the floor.

"Well now," the smiling crewman said in a thick accent. "You both came a little bit early. No matter, say goodnight," he said, as his facial expression became unfriendly. Tom took a swing at the man's jaw, but he easily stepped aside and slapped him with the back of his hand. Tom was hurled across the room and hit the wall. Shelia, without any thought, kicked the crewman in the belly, but it was like hitting a wall. The crewman grabbed Shelia and attempted to crush her throat.

"Nice try," the crewman said as he tightened his hand on Shelia's throat.

Tom recovered in time to grab the nearest chair and struck the crewman from behind as Shelia was at the point of blacking out. The crewman brushed off the chair and struck Tom across the chest with the palm of his hand. Tom's body flew over the captain's desk and landed on the floor. His hands tightened against his rib cage, holding his injured chest.

The captain's door opened, and a deep, loud voice cried out, "Party's over, folks." The crewman looked up to see a huge seven-foot-tall man towering over him and set himself in a combat stance. He struck Bert hard, but it had a very little effect. "I thought you might be one of those," and with all of Bert's strength, he struck the crewman's chest. The crewman sailed in the air and hit the wall, then dropped to the floor in a sitting position.

The crewman knew he had only a few seconds to live, and sputtered out, "Who are you?" then died.

Shelia saw Bert strike the crewman and was about to ask but stopped when Bert said, "Look, you have to understand, I am an illegal." In a panic, Bert added, "I have to go," as he ran out of the room. Shelia, coughing from a nearly compressed throat, crawled to Tom, then heard the familiar sound of a stunner and she blacked out.

Shelia was sitting beside Tom on his sickbay bed, holding his hand. From behind, she recognized the heavy steps.

"How is he?" Bert asked.

"Tom is much better. His healing process is almost finished."

"And the captain?"

"His neck is still sore, but he is back on duty. Thank you for saving my life," Shelia said.

Bert replied with a shy expression. It was Tom who saved your life. I came into the room just as Tom hit the guy with the chair. Otherwise, your throat would have been crushed."

"Bert, there are questions I have to ask you."

Bert shook his head, "Not here. Let's try the mess hall first."

"Wait a minute," Shelia said as she bent over Tom's head and kissed him gently on the lips. "All right, Bert. Lead on."

In the back corner of the mess hall, Shelia studied Bert while he was eating his synthetic Italian spaghetti, then asked, "How old are you?"

"I am almost 17 years old," Bert replied.

No wonder he acts like a kid sometimes, Shelia thought. "How can you be 17, when you look like a pre-hold age of 35?"

"Remember when I told you back in the captain's office about me being illegal?"

"You mean to say, a med-illegal?"

Bert lowered his head and nodded.

Shelia knew as a nurse that a medical illegal was anyone who had their DNA genetically modified or combined with unnatural DNA before they were conceived. The Commonwealth authority is mandated to dispose of any young or old medical illegal.

"It's so pathetic because everyone is illegal," said Bert.

"Not really," said Shelia. "When DNA genetic correction became available to the general public, the average healthy person's DNA had over 5000 defective chromosomes that were made normal. Cancer and other diseases became things of the past. With a perfect genetic DNA structure, we all can keep our appearance between 35 and 40 until we reach 120, then our body quickly breaks down and dies."

"Why 120 years and not forever?" Bert asked.

"Nobody knows the answer," Shelia replied. "The religious world says that their mythical God set man's threshold age from 900 down to 120 years." She continued, "Tell me about yourself, Bert,"

"If I tell you about myself, your life might get complicated."

"My life is already complicated, Bert, but maybe I could help you."

His face nearly in tears, he said "I'm tired of running and looking over my shoulder. I didn't do anything wrong. Why can't they leave me alone?"

"I don't have the answer as to why the law is so strict, but I can't help unless you tell me about yourself."

"I don't know very much about myself, other than what Mama told me."

"Who is Mama?" Shelia asked.

"Mama was a private scrap salvager on the prison penal colony."

"How were you connected with Mama?"

"A genetic researcher, Doctor Morse, was convicted for performing illegal research on human bodies and was sentenced to the prison colony. The doctor got caught again setting up an illegal lab. They found me as a month-old baby and ordered an injection termination, but it didn't take. Mama heard me crying near the incinerator located next to her scrap yard. Mama stole me away and kept me for herself. Mama hid me until I was 15 years old when she turned 120. For the next six months, I was her caretaker until she died. I couldn't prove that Mama was my mother, so the local police became suspicious, and I was on the run. For the next year, I earned enough to pay for the passage and a false identity. And here I am," Bert said bitterly.

"The man who nearly killed me, who is he?"

"He is not one of us," Bert replied.

"I don't understand," said Shelia.

"You must have noticed; he had an ungodly strength?"

"And so do you and maybe an even greater strength, Bert!"

"Ya, I know. Two weeks ago, two of them tricked me by inserting a compliance drug in my drink. They severely underestimated the drug dosage, and all it did was make me drowsy. I overheard their conversation about conditioning me to be a sleeper agent. I was scared and shouted, 'Not in your life!' I never saw anyone move so fast, and I slugged the first one in the head. He should have been knocked out cold, but all I did was make him mad. The second guy tried to grab my throat, but I crushed his hand instead. You should have seen the shock on his face. Then I got scared; I knew they were not human. When I am scared, I am really strong. I slugged the first guy again and heard his neck break. The second guy I hit in the chest like that other guy in the captain's room. With two dead unreal humans, I knew it was time to go off-world."

"But why do you call them unreal humans?" Shelia asked.

"I don't know; they just aren't real," Bert replied.

"One last question: how did you drop in the captain's room at the right time?"

"The crew members told me that the captain has never been known for his generosity, so I knew something was wrong when you were led to the boss's quarters instead of the captain's quarters."

"Thank you, Bert, and don't worry, your secret is safe with us."

***

Shelia and Bert stood in line at the Midway customs inspection. Bert couldn't help but notice Shelia was feeling nervous at Tom's absence.

"Hey, don't worry about Tom. He's not going to abandon you anytime soon," Bert remarked.

"If Tom doesn't hurry, the ship will soon leave us behind," Shelia said anxiously.

"Looking for somebody?" Tom announced himself with a smile.

Shelia felt relieved but wasn't about to let Tom off easy. "Where have you been?"

Tom answered, "The captain wanted me to join him in the boss's office and let him do all the talking."

"Why at the last minute?" Shelia asked.

"The captain feels that I deserve compensation for saving the ship and him, but the boss has a reputation for arrogance and stinginess. The captain gave him an ultimatum. He said 'Compensate Tom, or he will jump ship.' The boss said, 'Fine; you may go off-ship.' It was obvious; the boss was calling his bluff."

"The boss would call it a bluff," said Bert. "There isn't a captain anywhere who would work for the boss. Nor would any other ship owner hire the captain."

"Why wouldn't they hire the captain?" Shelia asked.

"The captain is a former pirate," Bert replied.

Tom nodded his head and continued with his story:

"Okay, we are going off-ship," the captain said. "By the way, the Commonwealth Authorities asked me to drop by their office about the disturbance aboard your ship."

"How did the Commonwealth find out about this?" the boss said in anger.

"I do not know," the captain replied, "but they told me you have also been requested an interview."

The boss stared at the captain, then checked his computer. "You are right, I did receive a request," the boss muttered.

"Once they find out about the bridge computer being vandalized and the attempted murder, this ship will be locked down and investigated. We aren't going anywhere for quite some time. Of course, the interview doesn't have to be complicated. As captain, I can take your place, and Tom can be quite absent-minded," the captain smiled.

"I get your point, Captain," the boss snarled. "How much is this going to cost me?"

"Here is the disc, all it needs is your approval."

The boss took the disc and inserted it into his computer. The boss sighed when he read the amount to be transferred.

"Okay, you win. Done," the boss said.

"Thanks, Boss. I will be back as soon as the Commonwealth lets me go. Come on, Tom."

"When the door closed behind us, I asked the captain, 'Look, I appreciate what you did back there, but why?' His answer was something I didn't expect to hear."

"What did the captain say?" Shelia asked anxiously.

"Your identification," the customs officer asked.

***

"This is incredible, I could be here forever and not get tired of this view," said Shelia. Tom and Shelia sat on the balcony chairs, overlooking the underground cavern. Tom sat quietly and nodded his head in agreement. Shelia felt apprehension about Tom, who was lost in thought, and asked, "Are you okay? You haven't said much since we left the customs office." Bert stepped onto the balcony and set the food tray on the table before them.

"You are right; I have several things on my mind that need to be cleared up. Bert, the credit that has been transferred to my account belongs to you."

Bert replied slyly, "Hey, Tom, why don't we split it three ways?"

Shelia cut in, "I'll go along with that idea. How much is it?"

"There are one thousand, three hundred and fifty credits for each of us," Tom replied.

Shelia's eyes widened, "That's enough for all three of us to buy our flat!"

"Maybe for you two, but not for me," said Bert. "I'm still illegal, and someday the medical staff will be suspicious of my modified DNA. That's when I move off-world."

"What is the other thing on your mind?" Shelia asked.

"When the captain was convicted for piracy and released from prison, he was blacklisted from being hired off-world, and all he could find for work was ground crew jobs for the cargo haulers. Many years later, a merchant trader felt sorry for him and hired him to work for the boss. The merchant trader said to the captain, "Do the Christian thing: do unto others as I do unto you."

"Who was the merchant trader," Shelia asked.

"Her name was Katherine Astern Styler, your mother."

***

Chapter 8

Shelia sat on a beach towel near the lake shore with Tom's head on her lap as they watched a blue and white parrot-like bird perch in a tree nearby.

"Shelia, how are you feeling today?" Tom asked.

"I still feel strange. Not sick, but different. When I looked in the mirror this morning, I was so certain that my skin was getting lighter. I am turning into Crystal, aren't I?"

Tom felt something fall on his cheek, and he picked it off with his fingers to study it. It was a brown-colored contact lens. Tom looked at Shelia and saw a blue color replace the brown eyes; only the other eye was still brown. Then, the other brown contact lens popped out. "Your brown contact lenses have popped out; now your eyes are blue. Your body rejected the lens fusion. I noticed something else; the roots of your hair are a lighter color, Ashburn blond."

"How am I going to explain this to everyone? I am Crystal; Shelia is a fake. Only, I still have only Shelia's memories." Shelia was about to get up and walk away when Bert showed up.

"Hello, Bert. You look as if you are leaving town."

"I am. I came to say goodbye."

"I thought you liked it here," said Tom.

"Haven't you heard? It's been 12 months now since the war started, and the Commonwealth Navy is doing mandatory selective drafting for recruits."

"I thought we won the war," Shelia said.

"There are still Thracian renegades out there that the Navy has to deal with. I am leaving before they find out the truth about me."

"How are you going off-world?" Shelia asked.

"I signed a one-year contract on the fanciest merchant trader ship I ever saw."

"Then we might as well come with you to see you off." They took public transport and stopped at the commercial wall entrance, which led to the elevator. The elevator took them upward until they arrived at the ship-holding chamber near the surface.

"There it is, the *Nyfodte*, an old-Earth Norwegian word for 'newborn,'" Bert said proudly.

"How did you find this ship?" Tom asked.

"I met one of their crewmen, and we became good friends," Bert said shyly.

"A lady friend?" Shelia said, smiling.

"Here she comes now," said Bert. "Hi, Tanya. I'd like you to meet my friends."

Tanya's smile turned to a look of complete shock. "Oh my gosh! "Please don't go away. Bert, make sure your friend doesn't go away," as Tanya ran back to the ship.

Tom saw the surprise on Shelia's face and understood that there was recognition between them. A small group rushed out of the ship and stood before Shelia. A tall, slim man cried out her name, "Shelia!"

Shelia's body violently shook, and tears ran down her face. She screamed, "No, you are not my father!" and fell unconscious into Tom's arms.

***

Jayson sat in a chair facing Tom a short distance away and said, "I assure you, Crystal is in good hands; Doctor Shan is a leading medical neurologist. If anyone can remove the memory block, it's him."

Tom looked around the hospital lobby and realized that more of her family were nearby. "It's not the memory block I am worried about. What will happen when Crystal is back and Shelia is gone? What will become of us?"

Jayson replied, "Doctor Shan told me that the memory block was only meant to last two weeks. Instead, the blockage has continued for over a year. There will be a merging of the two memory personalities. As for what her feelings are for you, I can't answer that one. Which of the two personalities would have the greater impact on her outlook? It depends on who has the stronger personality. Crystal is a very complex lady, and all I can say is that you should have faith that everything is in God's hands."

"Who is this woman, Shelia?" Tom asked.

Jayson sighed, then replied, "Shelia is Doctor Shan's late daughter who was assassinated. Shelia was standing next to my father when a sniper hit them both. Shelia was one of Crystal's closest friends, so there would be some confusion and bewilderment about the shared memories. Crystal by far is the stronger of the two. Therefore, it's my opinion that it will be Crystal, not Shelia, that will come out of that room."

"What does Doctor Shan think will happen?"

"The same as me, but the doctor thinks that Crystal's personality will mellow somewhat."

"What does he mean by that?"

Jayson smiled and replied, "Crystal is a very intelligent and headstrong young lady. Crystal has two bad traits: she is sarcastic like her father but much more so, and she also has a very bad temper. Shelia, on the other hand, rarely got angry and was more of a proper lady than Crystal. She has her mother's compassion for underdogs. I don't just mean homo sapiens, but any other sentient creature. And like her father, Crystal knows how to communicate and get on their good side."

"It sounds like her father is an interesting guy to know."

Jayson nodded, "I once had a one-year contract with Mark, and he taught me a lot: how to trade and also how to get along with the best and worst of the traders out there. Katherine, Crystal's mother, took my place after my contract was over. They were married for eighteen years before Katherine died. Then, five years ago, Mark and his ship, the *Marvel*, disappeared."

Tom suddenly felt uneasy and tried to change the subject, "What about you and your family?"

Jayson smiled, then replied, "Our ship is nearly finished being renovated, inside and out. The ship is outfitted as a private merchant ship but has a long-term contract with Midway. We will be a family-operated business, and Midway will be our home base. My one year with Mark has proven to be a valuable entrepreneurial business opportunity. Your friend Bert is one of the newest crew members. Also, my niece took a liking to him," Jayson smiled.

"Don't worry, I know about his background. The director changed his identity so that it says he was born here, and his parents abandoned him when he was a baby. I am also sorry to learn about your mother, Sheba. Did you know that she is my godmother?"

"No," Tom said as he looked up in surprise. "I did not know that. I guess you've got everything planned out, and your family's future is secured."

"Not entirely. There are always unknown factors, and you and Crystal are a couple of them. What is your relationship with Crystal?"

Tom closed his eyes, sighed, and whispered, "To be honest, I don't know. For one, who will Crystal be when she comes out of that room behind us? That scares the heck out of me."

"And the other?" Jayson asked. Tom was interrupted when the nurse exited Crystal's room.

"Mr. Steiner," the nurse smiled. "Doctor McGee has successfully released the memory block. The doctor will be joining you shortly."

"Thank you," Tom said. Tom heard the door open, and Doctor Shan, looking tired, sat down beside him.

"We were lucky. You mentioned that Doctor Halley was the one who changed the signature on the memory block. We were both on the same medical staff, and I recognized his signature, so I was able to remove the blockage code. Crystal is doing well, and she requested her uncle Jayson first before seeing you. I will be in my office if you wish to see me."

"Does Crystal seem angry?" Jayson asked.

"She doesn't appear to be," the doctor replied.

"Good. I won't be very long, Tom."

Tom had been waiting a few minutes when Jayson stepped out of the room with a strained but composed face. In a harsh voice, he said, "It's your turn, Tom," and he walked down the hallway with his hand over his stomach.

That must have been a big wallop to Jayson's stomach, Tom thought. He grinned as he entered Crystal's room to see her in bed, smiling at him. Crystal moved herself to one side of the bed and patted the sheet.

Tom laid down beside her and asked, "Would you slug me in the stomach if I told you, 'I love you?'"

"No, but I will do this," Crystal said as she rolled over to face Tom, and gave him the most passionate hug and kiss.

***

Tom sat next to Crystal in the Midway director's office and asked in a soft voice, "When was the last time you met your great-grandmother?"

"I never met her," said Crystal. "Uncle Jayson was only a young lad the last time he saw her. But they have kept in contact over the years. Did Uncle Jayson tell you what has happened with our family back home?"

"I knew a broad description of your home planet before we left the academy. Your uncle updated me with the details."

"Sorry for being late," a voice announced from behind. Tom and Crystal rose from their chairs to face the speaker.

"My, you do look like your mother," said Samantha. "Please sit down," she said as she sat across from them.

There is a family resemblance between the two ladies, Tom thought. *But Samantha has an air of authority about her.*

"Jayson told me that you both had quite an adventure. And Tom, you are very much like your mother, too."

"You knew my mother?"

"Only for a short while. Your mother wrote a story about our Midway project, but the Commonwealth put a cap on it."

"They are known for that," Tom said bitterly.

Samantha stared silently, nodded her head, and said, "If I could help you find your mother, I would. But if you should someday find her, Sheba is not going to recognize you."

"I have her memory bank," said Tom.

"Tom is a private contractor cryptologic technician for Commonwealth Navy Security; that's how he was able to gather the data."

Samantha smiled with increased respect for Tom. "Perhaps Tom, you should fill me in on the details."

"Oh, look at the time. I am due to be on shift at the medical clinic," said Crystal.

"I think it's a good idea for now for you to keep using Shelia's name until we can provide proper clearance for you. If you don't mind, I would like to talk with Tom for a little while longer."

"Sure, I'll see you later," Crystal said as she kissed Tom goodbye.

When Crystal left the office, Samantha let out a sigh and said, "You haven't been entirely honest with Crystal, have you?"

Tom, not sure how to respond, asked, "Why do you say that?"

Samantha restrained herself from losing her temper and replied, "I have dealt with all kinds of people, from sleazy politicians and royal elites to business people. I have learned their body language and voice patterns, and I have learned from their past and their reputations. You are hiding something from Crystal, and it is not good!"

Tom closed his eyes, trying hard not to show his emotions on his face. "If I tell Crystal the truth about my father, I may lose her for good."

Samantha rose from her chair and sat beside Tom. In a gentle voice, Samantha said, "You can't hold back the truth from Crystal forever."

"I know, but the timing is not right yet."

"When is it the right time?"

"I am leaving that in God's hands," Tom replied.

"Before you ask Crystal for her hand in marriage, I hope."

Tom nodded his head.

"What is the truth about your father?"

Tom leaned back in his chair and said, "How would Crystal feel about me and us when she finds out my father, Rear Admiral T. S. Melnyk, murdered Crystal's father, Captain Mark Styler, and his crew on the *Marvel*?"

Samantha silently stared at Tom, leaned back, raised her legs, and rested them on the opposite chair. After a few moments, she replied, "Your God better come up with a pretty good plan."

"Are you going to tell Crystal about my father?"

"I won't under one condition," said Samantha. "You tell Crystal the truth before you ask her to marry you."

"I promise," said Tom.

***

Tom, exhausted, exited the airlock and entered the hallway along with the rest of the survey crew. Tom removed this helmet and sat on the bench to remove his vacuum suit. The team leader walked up to Tom and sat beside him.

"Are you okay, Tom? You have been quiet all day today."

"I have a lot on my mind lately."

"Well, I want to thank you for your help in mapping the next cavern. You have been a great help. I hope to see you next week."

Tom nodded his head and was walking out of the changing room when a com overhead announced, "Mr. Beegle, please report to the Midway director's office. Miss Stevenson awaits your presence."

"Acknowledged. I am on my way," Tom replied. Tom, puzzled by the change of events, could only hope something interesting was waiting at the director's office. A singular public transport pod reserved with his name appeared above the door. Tom entered and sat on the single seat that was designed for comfort. *This luxury pod is going to cost the director a large number of credits*, Tom thought. The route took them through the solid iron tunnel, which was 40 miles long. The journey took only five minutes and stopped at a series of elevators. Tom exited the pod and wondered which elevator to take when one of the elevator doors opened.

"Mr. Beegle, please enter lift number four." Although it took only a minute, it seemed much too long.

"Computer, why is this lift taking so long?"

"Your journey is two and a half miles high; this lift will stop in another two minutes."

"I thought the director's office was only a half mile up."

"Correct. This lift will arrive at the director's private suite, where Miss Samantha Stevenson awaits you."

Sure enough, the lift ended in two minutes, and the door opened. Tom exited the lift and walked along the short tunnel, which led to a single old-fashioned door with a handle.

"Please walk in, Mr. Beegle," the door announced.

Tom was about to turn the door lever as the door swung open. Tom smiled when Crystal stood before him. "Tom, I am so glad you made it here."

Crystal embraced Tom and shut the door behind him.

"What is going on here?" Tom whispered in Crystal's ear.

A grim look came over Crystal's face, and she replied, "We have to leave again."

"Why? I thought we had a future here."

"You still can, but not for a while yet," said Samantha. "We were just about ready to have dinner. Make yourself comfortable and enjoy the view."

Beyond the kitchen, dining room, and living room was a floor-to-ceiling glass window showing them an incredible view, as it overlooked the 40-mile-long cavern. It was two and a half miles to the floor and almost another mile up to the ceiling. The twin rows of lights along the ceiling were starting to dim for the night. A cloud along the ceiling was beginning to form. Later in the evening, it would produce a fine mist below.

"Dinner is ready," Crystal announced.

Tom was disappointed as he walked away from the glass wall and sat beside Crystal.

"Tom, could you say grace for us, please?" said Samantha.

***

"I still don't get it; with my false identification, I am hardly qualified for the military draft."

"I agree, but your name is high on their list. Once they find out your real identity, there is no telling what might happen to you. There isn't much time for you to get off-world. Jayson's ship has already left Midway and won't be back for three weeks. You need to keep a low profile for at least a year before it's safe to come back to Midway. By then, the draft should be over."

"That's a long time to be separated from you, Crystal."

"Not very likely; I'm coming with you!"

"You may have to. Your appearance has changed, making it more likely you will be picked up by the Commonwealth authorities."

"Do you have any suggestions for us, Samantha?"

"I think so," Samantha said as she rose from her sofa. "Room Computer," Samantha commanded, "Engage the wall monitor." The glass wall window was converted into a monitor. "Open file sector 5-13." A star map of the territorial Sector 5 appeared on the monitor.

"Midway, as you already know, is located between Sector Two and territory Sector Five. A solar system called 'Alliance' is 13 light-years away in Sector Five. The fourth planet, Green Shield, is presently manned by a small private exploration contractor for the Commonwealth. Their assignment is to map the planet's resources and consider possible future immigration. The person in charge of the operation is here on Midway, a dear old friend of mine. His name is Tony, and he is looking for a starship pilot. I convinced Tony to hire Crystal for a one-year contract."

"I knew Crystal could pilot a flitter, but a starship?"

"Tom, I started flying the *Marvel* when I was 13 and got my pilot's certificate when I turned 16." Crystal smiled.

"But you need an interfaced ship computer implant to get your pilot's certificate!"

"I have that, too," Crystal added. "My father had very resourceful connections with the right people."

"Okay, so we have a qualified pilot. What about me?" Tom asked.

"You have some experience as a surveyor," said Samantha.

"And you are a genius with the computer, too," Crystal smiled.

"Tony will meet you at the West Sub-Level Terminal Lobby 5. Be there in the lobby no later than two hours from now."

"Then we'd better leave now and pick up my stuff at my suite."

"It's too risky; they may be looking for you tonight," said Samantha.

"I have no choice; my mother's memory is hidden in my room."

"Oh dear, I forgot about that. All right, but please be careful and good luck. One more thing, Tom, don't forget about your father," Samantha warned.

Tom silently stared at Samantha. "I promise," Tom replied.

"What promise?" Crystal asked.

"There is no time for that," said Tom. "I will tell you after we are off-world."

Tom gathered all his devices and inserted them into the hidden jacket pouches. The electronic notepad and clothes were placed in his duffel bag. Crystal, dressed in the spacer coveralls, entered the suite with her duffel bag.

"I'm ready to go. How about you?" Shelia asked.

"Just one more thing," Tom said as he took the picture off the wall and removed a flat silver object behind it.

"My mother's memory data." Tom put the memory data securely in his waist pouch. Then, the door charm startled them.

"Were you expecting somebody tonight?" Shelia asked.

"No, I wasn't." Tom opened the door.

"Hi Tom, Shelia, remember me?"

"Oh..." Tom groaned to himself. "It's Allen in a Navy uniform."

"Hey Allen, it's great to see you again, but Shelia and I are going hiking."

"Nice try, Tom, but I think you are both leaving town," said Allen. "Nobody goes hiking when it's almost dark outside. Are you going to invite me in, or do I have to call for backup?"

"Backup?"

"I work for the Navy now as a recruiter."

Tom sighed and said, "Come on in."

"Hey, you have a nice suite here. Not bad for a surveyor." Allen sat down on the sofa with his hands behind his head. "Shelia, do me a favour and pour me a drink."

"Stuff it, Allen. Why are you here?"

"Crystal, please..." Tom pleaded.

"Tom, he is no fool, and he is playing with you. What do you want, Allen?" Crystal demanded.

"Oh, now it's Crystal. This is getting more interesting."

"How did you find us, Allen?"

"As I said, I am a recruiter for the Navy. My job is to select whomever I want, whenever I want. I looked up the single personal profiles on Midway when I saw your picture with a different name. Naturally, I got curious and would like to hear your story first."

"Allen, you have known me for a long time. Anything I would say would be a cover-up or a lie," Tom said.

Allen laughed, then replied, "True. Oh, so true."

"I am not so sure I understand what you guys are talking about," said Crystal.

"I guess Crystal doesn't know about us?"

"What is Allen talking about Tom?"

Tom was straining to keep himself from exploding in anger, and he said nothing.

"I will tell you," said Allen. "Before Tom got hired on as a private contractor with the Navy Security, which is almost unheard of anywhere else, he was a hacker. The best hacker on the Academy; is probably the best hacker anywhere in this pathetic universe. When Tom went missing, I thought it was time for me to disconnect with security. I heard there was an opening for a recruiter, and here I am."

"Okay, that's enough. You didn't come for a friendly chat. What do you want from us?"

"Two thousand credits," Allen replied.

"What? We don't have that kind of credit," Crystal cried.

"You may not, but Tom does."

"Allen, those credits are locked on Academy under my mother's name."

"Nice try. You also have the co-joint password and your signature, and thumbprint." Allen slipped out his digital pocket notebook from the jacket and set it on the table between them. "Release the three codes, and you will not hear from me again."

"I don't trust him, Tom!"

"I understand you're concerned, but he's got me cornered. All right, you win."

Tom picked up the notepad from the table and set it on his left knee. Tom removed the silver electronic-pen from his shirt pocket and clicked it on. "Darn it; the charge is depleted. Do you have a charger on you, Allen?"

"You bet, give me your e-pen."

Tom threw the e-pen over to Allen, and as he grabbed it in his hand, he let out a small cry and fell unconscious to the floor.

"What happened to Allen?" Crystal asked in astonishment.

Tom reached for his pen and slipped it back into his shirt pocket. "My stunner is disguised as a pen; it is only good for one charge."

"But, how did your stunner pass through all the port terminal scanners?"

"Other than the appearance of the pen, there is no self-contained battery or built-in charger unit. You need an external wireless charger to make the stunner work. Allen has a wireless charger on his belt clip for all his electronic devices.

We are running out of time, but I need to do one more thing with Allen."

Tom picked up Allen's notepad and turned on his recorder. "Hello, Allen, just a short note. I recorded our conversation about your attempted blackmail. By the time you wake up, we will be long gone. If you tag us with Navy Security, I will release the video of your disastrous performance. Sweet dreams, Allen. And one more thing—never play games with your tutor. Out. Okay, let's go."

***

"Prepare for a warp jump in 5, 4, 3, 2, 1. We are now in warp space," the ship's computer announced. "The estimated time to our destination is 3 to 5 days."

"I wish Sara was here," Crystal whispered.

"Who is Sara?" Tom asked.

Crystal, startled, said, "Don't sneak up on me like that!"

"Sorry, I didn't mean to spook you."

"You didn't...never mind; Sara is my pet name for our main computer on my father's ship, the *Marvel*. Tony, the ship is on auto, so may we be excused? I'd like to discuss some private issues with Tom in our quarters."

"Sure, go ahead and take your time. I've got nothing else to do."

Tom followed behind Crystal to their joint quarters. "If you don't mind, I will take the lower bunk," said Crystal.

"Not at all, I prefer the upper bunk. What do you want to talk about?" Tom said as he sat on one of the two chairs.

"Are you a hacker? And who is this father of yours?"

"Maybe we should start with my father. Today, he is known as Rear Admiral Steiner of the Commonwealth Navy Space Security."

"Wow, you must be proud of your father."

Tom replied, "No, my mother has described my father as arrogant, self-serving, and a sociopath."

"You mean a psychopath."

"No, a psychopath can be proven and screened out with a brain scan, a person becomes a sociopath through learned behaviour."

"I didn't know that. I guess you and your father don't get along very well?"

"I wouldn't know, I have never met my father, and he doesn't want anything to do with me. My mother doesn't want anything to do with him either. The two of them agreed through a third party; Mother received yearly child support."

"Why the secretive child support payments?"

"Crystal, the one-night stand wasn't consented to."

"Oh, sorry," said Crystal.

"It's okay; Mother got over it. At the time, my father was a commander and my mother was only an ensign, which was grounds for a court martial. After the child support agreement, Mother resigned from the Navy in the media department and worked for a local private media station. When I was growing up, I had a great bond with my mother but had no male role model to look up to. I became quite introverted and got mixed up with the local hackers. Things progressed from there. It didn't take long for me to advance beyond the local hackers' expertise. I started to design my own programs to enhance my hacking skills. When I was 17, I took advanced computer science and learned to become a cryptologic technician."

"I thought you had to be in the Navy to become a cryptologic technician." Tom silently smiled at Crystal. "Oh, I see. Go ahead."

"After my advanced education, I asked if my mother could help me get into the Navy Cryptologic Technician Department as an enlisted private contractor. By then, my father had been promoted to rear admiral."

"Your father agreed to this?"

"No, he didn't, so Mother blackmailed him. When I showed up on the following Monday, I took the Navy's introduction course, and things have just fit in place since then."

"So, what happened back there one year ago?"

Tom's face turned grim. "It's rather complex. It's not unusual for my mother to disappear for two or three days when she is hot on the news breaking a story. Mother was gone for a week, so I checked with her boss to see if she was okay. All I got from her boss was a scripted reply. That meant that Mother had been secretly arrested."

"My gut feeling was that the Navy Security was involved. The next day, while I was doing my regular assignment, I set up my program and a small, portable halo monitor. Afterward, I found the seal code for Mother's arrest and the authorized signature. The signature was my father's, but I nearly blew my cover and exited the security net. There was no way I could find where my mother was or what had happened to her. I needed help; that's why I contacted some of my hacker friends for assistance. One of the hackers found out that the description of a patient at the hospital fit my mother. She had had her mind wiped and was sent off-world. I had to get into the hospital mind section; it was the only way I could find out about my mother."

"Allen was the inside man at the hospital. Before I allowed myself to be caught snooping in my father's security department, Allen modified the skull cap at the hospital. My father's own personal goons arrested me, and they brought me to the mind department at the hospital, as I thought they would. It seems that Doctor Halley and my father have been working together for a long time on their agenda. When they thought the mind wipe and the false memory were successfully completed, they left the room. That's when I made my move. I found Mother's memory data and downloaded it to my memory card. I also found reference data associated with Mother's files."

"What was on that file is the promise I made to Samantha. I intended to tell you about my father, but I couldn't find the right time. I suppose this is as good a time as any," Tom said as he set the notepad on the table and opened the file. Crystal read the document three times before she turned off the notepad.

"I am very sorry," Tom said as he touched Crystal's shoulder.

"Don't you dare touch me!" Crystal yelled as she stood up from the chair. "You men are all the same! I have been manipulated, deceived, and lied to by my grandfather, my uncle, two doctors, and now you," Crystal shouted.

"Crystal, I didn't..."

"Shut up! I am not finished. Let me make this clear, from now on, anything between us is just business! Am I making this clear to you? It's just business between us! And for the record, I would have never kept a secret from you or deceived anyone."

Crystal turned around as she stormed out of the quarters. Crystal walked past Tony and sat down hard on the pilot chair. "Men! They are the most arrogant, pathetic, and idiotic…"

"Ah, Crystal, I would like to inform you about the contract regarding any misconduct on this ship."

Crystal turned to face Tony with a silent, red, deadly glare. Tony quickly realized he was on dangerous ground, and said, "If you excuse me, I have something important to do," as he left the bridge. "I just remembered why I am still single," Tony whispered.

It was past her shift when Crystal looked at the time and decided it was time to call it a night. Crystal entered the darkened quarters, quickly undressed, and slipped under the bed sheets. Sometime later, Crystal had to ask Tom a question.

"Tom, are you awake?"

"Yes," Tom replied.

"Why did your father murder my father?"

"I truly don't know."

"Truly?"

"Yes!" Tom replied.

"I have another question: How do I know you are not like your father?"

"I guess it's possible, but Mother and I took a different approach to life."

"What do you mean by that?"

"Before I went in for advanced education, I was not only introverted but an angry and rebellious teenager."

"It sounds like we've got more in common than we think. Never mind, continue."

"Mother and I started on Bible studies, and things just progressed from there."

"So, what did you gain by praying to your God?"

"Nothing! But I can tell you this: I lost my anger, ego, greed, and insecurity. Sometimes, it's not gaining, but losing, which in itself is gaining. What do you mean, we have more in common?"

"Night," Crystal said as she felt tears on her face.

Chapter 9

Crystal guided the surveyorship through the thick, clouded atmosphere of the planet Green Shield. The ship flew below the low-lying clouds, and she could see the planet surface. The planet had a few mountain ranges and was covered with vast, endless green, treeless plains and valleys. Lakes and rivers were extremely rare, and the few small patches of rough ground exposed grey rocks.

"Tony, why is the daylight side of this planet completely covered by clouds and not the night side?" Shelia asked.

"In this solar system, the eighth planet is a dwarf brown sun. For millions of years, Planet Green Shield was bombarded by the sun's cosmic rays, causing the extremely clouded formation on the dayside. That is why you will never see the sun or a blue sky. At night, the cloud disperses, revealing the stars. The atmosphere's temperature is moderate, and rainstorms are quite rare. The morning mists and dew water the plants. Hundreds of millions of years ago, the brown sun's cosmic rays were so strong that they caused the clouds to thicken and lower the temperature. The planet was completely covered with ice. As the brown sun aged, the cosmic rays drastically reduced, and the glacier ice ball dispersed, leaving behind the eroded mountains and vast plains. Most of the low-eroded mountain range is grey shale, and the soil everywhere else is dark silt. Vast plains, plateaus, and low valleys surround this range. There is a lot of wildlife, but most of them will keep their distance from us. There is not much variety in colour, as the plants and wildlife come in different shades of green. Even the clouds have a slight shade of green, which is why we call this planet 'Green Shield'."

"How did the vegetation and wildlife come into existence?" Tom asked.

"That is one of the reasons the Commonwealth sent us here—to find the answer," Tony replied.

"Any intelligent life down there?" Shelia asked.

"Just the Rexes!"

"Rexes?" Tom asked.

"There is the outpost research station," said Tony. "You can land anywhere on the south side."

Crystal could see that the outpost consisted of 12 portable domes of various sizes, none larger than 30 feet wide. The outpost was positioned in the plain near a bluff, facing the north.

"How many personnel are within this outpost?" Crystal asked.

"Ten, including us three," replied Tony.

"You don't have a flitter," Crystal said as she landed the starship.

Tony shyly replied, "We are a low-budget operation. But we do have six bike floaters, and every year, we load up everything on the ship and move to a new campsite."

"When are you moving the outpost again?" Crystal asked.

"About five months from now. Here come the guys," said Tony.

"All men, no women?" Crystal asked.

"We did have one woman, but she died in an accident."

"What caused the accident?" Crystal asked.

"She fell off a bike floater and broke her neck."

"Nine guys and one woman," Crystal muttered.

"Okay. Let's unpack the cargo haul," said Tony.

Crystal opened the cargo door to face a group of seven men, who stared back in silence.

Tony broke the silence and said, "You want your stuff or not?"

The men quickly introduced themselves, then passed by Crystal to gather their things.

"Tony," said Crystal with a forced smile, "when was the last time these guys saw a woman?"

Tony hesitated before answering, "Two years."

"Tony, you have two choices: either I beat you to a pulp here and now or you will inform everyone that Tom is my devoted husband, we work together, and he is a little crazy. Got it?"

"Ya, sure, no problem. As soon as we finish unloading the ship, I will mention to the guys that you and Tom are married."

"And don't forget, a little crazy, too," Crystal demanded.

"Right, a little crazy, too," said Tony.

"Thank you, Tony," said Crystal with a warning glare. Crystal turned and noticed Tom had overheard their conversation.

"Just remember, it's still business between us," she said as she marched out to the domes.

***

Three bike floaters glided through the green, grassy savannah, each leaving behind a trail of depressed grass, and came to a stop. Crystal stepped off the bike and saw a large, shallow depression that extended far into the horizon. Crystal was fascinated by the vast, rolling savannah that surrounded them. The knee-high sea of grass moved in complex motion with the air currents. Not a single animal disturbed the magic of the scenery except for a green-coloured flock of birds that flew high across the sky. The birds were too high in the sky to make out their type.

Jon, the biologist, released a drone in the air as it searched the area. The drone soon disappeared over the horizon.

"The drone has indicated on my notepad that several different herds of Rexes are nearby," said Jon.

"We haven't seen the Rexes yet; I would like to see them," said Crystal.

"Sure, why not? But we have to keep a low profile when observing them. I will bring back the drone now. Then, we can park our bikes near the bluff just ahead."

When the drone returned, Jon placed it back in the bike's rear storage compartment. After they parked their bikes, they slowly crawled on top of the bluff. Several large herds of animals similar to antelopes were quietly munching on the grass.

"Where are the Rexes?" Crystal whispered in excitement.

"The Rexes are hidden in the grass. Because of the downdraft from the wind, the herds can't smell them."

Crystal pulled out her binoculars and focused on the herds. The animals resembled Earth's waist-high antelopes, but they had a green body that was perfectly camouflaged by the grass. Suddenly, the herd scattered in every direction as a dozen Rexes jumped up and grabbed the antelopes by their necks. The short, powerful arms of the rexes' biped bodies quickly crushed the antelopes' necks. In a few seconds, six antelope lay dead.

Crystal focused the binoculars on the Rexes and was surprised by what she saw. Crystal lowered the binoculars and said, "They are like the Tyrannosaurus!"

"Not really," said Jon. "They are mammals, not lizards. Their heads are similar, but their teeth are like ours. The Rexes arms are larger than the Tyrannosaurus, and their body is covered with short green matted fur. They also have a much larger brain cavity. That's why we to shorten the name 'Rexes'. And the Rexes are smart-very smart. We had to raise the security shield around our outpost because they kept raiding our compound looking for things to steal."

"How tall are the Rexes?" Tom inquired.

"They range from six to seven feet in height. So far, they have not attacked us. Except perhaps for Genet."

"I thought she broke her neck when she fell off her bike," said Tom.

"That's true, but she was being chased by the Rexes at the time. The Rexes never touched her when they caught up with her."

"How do you know all this?" Crystal asked.

"Her probe recorded it all. Let's head back to the outpost," Jon said quickly. Without another word, Jon hopped on the bike and left them behind.

"What is with Jon?" Tom asked.

"I think Genet must have been his friend, or maybe his wife."

"If that is true, why did Jon stick around?" Tom wondered.

"Another mystery to solve, I suppose."

"Crystal, it's been several weeks. Can we talk?"

"No," Crystal replied as she rode her bike to hurry after Jon.

Tom sighed and followed behind her.

***

"Good morning, Tom and Crystal. You folks have been assigned to Karl today," said Tony. "I will leave it to Karl to fill you in on the details."

"We are going to do something different this week," Karl said.

"As a geologist, I am curious about some small metallic contents detected by our sensors near the small mountain range south of here. This is a young planet, and most of the mountains are made of slate materials. It's a two-day journey, and we may be there for a week, so let's load up enough supplies on a floater cart. I want to leave no later than noon," he said as he got up and exited the room.

Crystal and Tom stared at each other. "Let's do what the man says," Tom smiled.

"You can go first; I want to finish my coffee," said Crystal.

"Okay, I'll meet you later at the bikes."

When Crystal was alone, Jon wandered in and saw Crystal sitting alone. "Do you mind if I join you?" Jon said as he sat down across from Crystal.

Crystal, annoyed by having her personal space invaded, replied instead, "Who is Genet?"

"I don't know."

"What do you mean, you don't know? Tony told me you and Genet spent the most time together."

"You and Tom are new here. Our payroll is not great, so why do you think we are all here in this backward world? Your payroll is no different from ours, so I'm guessing you and Tom are here for the same thing as us. We are all hiding from the authorities. Am I right?" Jon asked.

Crystal, caught off guard by this sudden change of events, replied, "Why are you here?"

"I just told you, I am hiding, just like you. We all have our little secrets, including Genet."

Crystal, feeling nervous, said, "If you'll excuse me, I need to get ready," as she stood up to leave.

"Sure. See you when you get back from your trip," said Jon.

Why does that man give me the creeps? Crystal thought as she spotted Tony a short distance away.

"Tony!" Crystal shouted. "Wait right there."

From the look on Crystal's face, he knew trouble was brewing again.

"Why didn't you tell me your crew is all misfits?" Crystal asked.

"They are no better or worse than your Tom, a draft dodger."

"He's not a draft dodger. An idiot conned him."

"So were the rest of us," said Tony defiantly.

Crystal, puzzled, asked, "What do you mean?"

"One is a political advocate, a scapegoat for tax fraud, and another was facing a court martial for refusing orders."

"What was Genet hiding from?"

"Genet came across something that would warrant a mind wipe or death."

"What was it?" Crystal asked.

"I don't know; it was for our sake that Genet kept it a secret."

"Okay... Ah, Tony, sorry for being so hard on you."

"It's all right; Samantha told me what would happen."

***

Crystal was not the slightest bit tired of sightseeing after two days of watching endless savannahs and the various wildlife feeding on the grasses. *It's so peaceful viewing the scenery on this noiseless floater*, she thought.

"There it is," Karl pointed out.

Crystal lifted the binoculars to her eyes and saw the low grey mountain range. The mountains had the same eroded look as the other mountains on the planet. They were all composed of the same black and grey slate material, which created a sharp contrast with the green surroundings.

"When we arrive at the foothills, we will turn west and follow the river. The savannah will gradually be replaced by trees, which will hamper our bikes' speed, and we will have to slow down."

Crystal was the first to arrive at the ridge where the river lay as the water flowed west. As Karl instructed, she turned west along the ridge, and they eventually arrived at their destination.

"It's somewhere around here; I am releasing the drone," said Karl.

Karl removed the drone and released it into the atmosphere. The drone made a wide circular pattern, and its scanner detected a metallic source. "It is an old Imperial yacht," said Karl. "Or what is left of it? I am bringing back the drone."

"What is the yacht doing out here?" Tom inquired.

"There were a lot of missing Imperial yachts before the Commonwealth installed the repeater to safely guide the ships in warp space to their final destinations," said Crystal.

"Here it comes. That's odd; the drone suffered a malfunction. It's still coming back, though." The drone flew unevenly toward Karl, and he caught it in his hand.

"Do you want me to examine it?" Tom asked.

"After we investigate the ruin," said Karl. "All right, let's take our bikes and cross the river."

Crossing the river was the easy part, Crystal thought, as they drove around the trees and boulders, slowing down their journey until they arrived at the ruins.

"It doesn't look like there will be any survivors, but keep your eyes open for any signs of life," said Karl.

Crystal walked straight for the ship's bridge, but it was completely wrecked. Crystal left the bridge and found Tom in the gallery.

"The food locker is empty, and the quarters have been cleaned out. Perhaps there will be survivors. Did you find anything interesting on the bridge?"

"No, there is nothing salvageable. This ship is old, but it doesn't seem like it crashed here all that long ago," said Crystal.

"Karl is in the engine room. He wants to see if we can salvage the drive pile."

"You can forget that idea," said Karl as he came walking up the gallery. "Most of the drive pile is destroyed, yet the others are missing."

"This is all very strange," said Tom. "There aren't any bodies, yet something is wrong here, and I can't put my finger on it. I want to examine the ship's computer on the bridge. You and Karl may want to search the area for any sign of survivors."

When Tom stepped onto the bridge, he couldn't fathom how anyone could have survived the impact. The destruction was total, with the ship's computer, navigation, recorder, and everything else in ruins, yet there were no bodies. Then it hit him: That's because there were never any humans on this ship!

Tom touched his comlink and said, "Crystal, Karl, return to the ship now!" There was no reply. Tom checked his stunner and set it on "narrow beam" to increase his range, though he thought it would probably do him little good. *This is not good,* Tom thought; *there is no way I can win this battle.* He looked around to see what else he could use as a weapon. He thought back to what Karl said about a missing drive pile. *The drive pile is used to power the ship. Of course, now I know why the drive pile is missing. And I think I know how to fight back.* Tom hoped he was right.

Hours later, the noise of metal scraping on metal could be heard echoing along the gallery. A red metallic robot was carrying a drive pile plate strapped to his midsection.

The robot called out, "I know you are on this ship. Your friends are not hurt, just immobile. You and your friends are too useful for me to destroy. Your stunner will not harm me, so you might as well give up."

The robot's voice stopped at the bridge entrance, and a new voice was heard. In the middle of the bridge, a wire attached to the ceiling held a pocket notepad. The voice came from the notepad, and it said, "I believe this is what you are looking for—this pen." Sure enough, a silver pen was hanging from the notepad.

"Why would I need this pen? It must be a trick." The robot used its sensor on the notepad and pen, and no explosive materials were detected. The robot searched the bridge and the rest of the ship, but he was alone. The robot entered the bridge again and reached for the pen.

An explosion sounded throughout the ship. After the debris settled, Tom carefully entered the bridge and saw the robot severed at the midsection. The robot's head slowly turned toward Tom.

"You were quite clever with your pen; I would never have thought the pen would create feedback and cause the ship's drive pile to explode."

"Where are my friends?" Tom demanded.

"Near the bikes. They have not been harmed, but they are unconscious. Now I shall return to where I belong," the robot said as the light went out of its eyes.

"What are you talking about?" Tom asked, but there was no reply because the robot was gone. Tom rushed out and headed for the bikes. He found Crystal and Karl.

Tom sat down beside Crystal and covered her with a blanket. When her eyes opened, Tom said, "How are you feeling?"

"Drowsy. What has happened?"

"You and Karl got hit by a stunner."

"Who did this?"

"You want the real story or the fake story?"

Crystal stared at Tom, then replied, "The real story, of course."

"The lone operator of that ship was one of Old Earth's rebel robots. But don't you worry, the robot is gone now."

"You defeated the robot, but how? They are hard to destroy."

"The robot's power source was depleted, and he was using the ship's drive pile plate, which was strapped to his midsection. I used my pen to send feedback to the drive pile plate and caused it to explode."

"So, what's the problem with the real story?" Crystal asked.

"In my years with the Navy Security, I learned about a secretive law, which is that having any knowledge on the robots warrants a mind wipe. If the public were to find out the robots were not destroyed 100 years ago, it would cause widespread panic."

"And what would be the fake story?" Crystal asked.

"The ship was operated by a lone, crazed man who shot both you and Karl from behind. We fought in hand-to-hand combat, and I killed him and won."

"Alright, but why are you telling me this?" Crystal asked.

"I realized that if there ever was going to be a future between us, then I needed to be honest with you. Karl should be awake very soon."

Tom rose from the ground and said, "You can tell Karl whatever story you choose. I am going to bury the robot or the lone man. It's your call, Crystal," Tom said as he walked back to the ship.

It was a long two-day journey back to the outpost, and neither Crystal nor Tom spoke much. They entered the compound weather-beaten and tired.

"I am heading to the office to file my report," said Tom, and he waited for Crystal's response.

Crystal, unsure of what to say, walked up to him. "I don't want to give you the impression that everything is okay now. I'm still trying to sort things out in my life and decide what to do about us. But I want to give you something."

"What is it?" Tom asked.

"This!" Crystal kissed Tom and quickly walked away.

Tom watched Crystal enter the dome. Tom stood alone for a few seconds, then said, "Thanks, I needed that."

Chapter 10

Crystal entered the mess hall, saw Tom sitting alone, and decided to join him. After Crystal had made her choices from the buffet, she walked towards Tom and sat across from him.

"Why are your eyes so baggy?" Crystal asked.

Tom replied, "I haven't slept very well for the past two days."

"Tom, you should know that I do appreciate what you did for me. I mean that with sincerity."

"Thanks, but it's not what kept me up," said Tom.

"Then what is it?"

Tom looked around to see if they were alone. "It's what that robot said before it died."

"Tom, robots don't die. They either cease to exist or are destroyed."

"Not this one; I think it was awakened?"

"Tom, that could be dangerous thinking. I've heard stories where people get hauled off for interrogation just for suggesting that. Some of them don't come back. What makes you sure this robot was awakened."

"I'm not completely sure, but what he said troubles me."

"Now you are referring to this robot as a 'he'? What did this robot say that shook you up so much?" Crystal asked.

"He, or it, said, 'I am finished. Now I can go back to where I belong'."

"I can see how those words could affect you, but you have to remember, it was nearly destroyed, and it could be an illusion."

"Maybe or maybe not, I guess we will never know," said Tom.

"Too much knowledge could be dangerous for your health, just like Genet. Tony told me the authorities were after her because she knew too much, and they wanted to perform a mind wipe on her. Tony didn't know anything else. Please be careful. I don't want anything to happen to you. I am finished with my meal, and there is a small chore I have to do. I'll see you later, Tom."

"Thanks for joining me for breakfast and for the warning."

Crystal nodded as she rose from her chair and left the room. Tom lifted his cup and noticed it was empty, then set it back on the table. "I suppose you are right; I need to forget what the robot said," Tom muttered.

Karl poked his head through the door and said, "Hey Tom, could you give me a hand, please?"

"On my way," said Tom.

***

Tom and Crystal stacked the last containers against the interior dome wall.

"Did Tony say where we are all moving?" Tom asked.

Crystal replied, "On the other side of the continental divide, about 950 miles southeast of here. It will be a nice change of scenery."

"What about this container? It is not the same as the others. What's inside it?" Crystal asked.

"I don't know. They were piled behind all the other containers. It's locked, but I should be able to fix that," said Tom.

Tom removed his pocket notepad and set it on top of the lock. The notepad auto detected the lock and analyzed the code. In a minute, the notepad had broken the code and released the lock.

"Where did you get this device?"

"Back during my hacker days, my hacker friends and I had a game: who can open the digital lock the fastest."

"Let me guess, you won," Crystal smiled.

Tom grinned and said, "Let's see what's inside the container."

"Oh, this is interesting; these must be Genet's possessions," said Crystal. "Why are Genet's things still here?"

"I guess Tony doesn't know what to do with them," said Tom. "There isn't much, really, mostly clothes, pictures, personal items, and a memory disc." Tom removed the disc and placed it in his pocket. "That's it. Let's see what else Tony wants done."

Later in the evening, Tom was so absorbed in analyzing Genet's memory disc that he didn't notice when a fresh cup of coffee was placed in front of him. Tom looked up to see Crystal staring at him with a concerned look.

"You need a break," Crystal suggested.

"I need to think over what I found," said Tom.

"You broke the code?" Crystal whispered.

"Yes, there are some documents and a small diary. This Genet was something else. Look at this picture of her and tell me what you think."

Crystal studied the picture. *She was certainly muscular for a woman*, she thought.

"Who does Genet remind you of?"

Crystal studied the photo for a moment, then replied, "That crewman who attacked us on the cargo ship when we boarded at the penal colony," Crystal cried. "Do you think Genet and that guy might be clones? Bert said the crewman's appearance was the same as the other two that kidnapped him on the penal colony. Tony is right; she was running away from the Commonwealth."

"You are half right. According to her diary, it wasn't the Commonwealth that was after her; it was the clones. But she called them 'the outsiders' and us 'the insiders.' This makes the story even more confusing. There is a small group of clones working together with our people. But something happened two years ago, and their plans fell apart. Their home base was destroyed, and it was every man and woman for themselves. There was an argument between the clones, and it looks like this Genet was a runaway."

"Who destroyed their home base?"

"The Thracian," Tom replied. "Here is what bothers me the most: who or what is their master? There are many masters, and sometimes they seem to be talking about themselves, and sometimes they do not."

"I am flaked out and tired. I am also tired of feeling alone," said Tom.

"You are not alone; I am here, too," Crystal protested.

"Are you? When I am too close, you always push me back." Tom rose and went to his bed. Too tired to undress, he laid down on his side to go to sleep.

"Tom, I have been hurt too many times in the past by people that were close to me. I am afraid that I am going to be hurt again," said Crystal.

Tom replied from the bed, "The truth is, everyone is going to hurt you. You've just got to find the ones that are worth suffering for."

Crystal watched Tom roll to his other side to face away from her. She got up and looked out the window, just as the faint outline of the sun disappeared over the horizon. She rested her forehead on the Plexiglas window and closed her eyes. After a while, Crystal turned her head toward the sleeping man across from her bed. She quietly tip-toed to his bed and looked down at him.

"Yes, you are worth suffering for," Crystal whispered as she lay down beside Tom and hugged him.

***

"Thank you, everyone, for all your help over the last six months," Tony said as he looked around, smiling.

"Tomorrow, we will load up and move to our next destination, which was originally 950 miles away but has since been changed. The Commonwealth has overridden our next operation and sent us to the other side of Green Shield, 12,000 miles away. Their probe has shown unusual land formations, and we are being sent to investigate. We leave tomorrow evening at 1800 hours."

"Tom and Crystal, I want you both to assist Jon in bringing in the malfunctioning sled floater. Jon will give you the details."

"That's it. Clean up begins at sunrise tomorrow," Tony said as he left the room.

"Hi guys," Jon said as he sat across from them. "It's an easy job. We will bring back the broken sled in time for supper. I would like to leave within an hour. See you later."

"We might as well get ready. You look lost in thought, Tom," said Crystal.

"I had the most amazing peace of mind last night," Tom shyly smiled.

Crystal smiled and said, "So did I."

***

Three bikes travelled along the grassy plain, with the last bike towing a sled. The usual cloudy weather never seemed to touch the surface, adding to the swirling movement of the sea of green grass. A short distance away, a huge herd of antelope foraged on the meadow.

Jon halted his bike as the others stopped beside him.

"This is incredible. There must be thousands of them," Crystal said in astonishment.

"The antelope are on a migration route from north to south, and the mating season has begun. After they give birth, the herd migrates back north until next year," said Jon. "We are almost there. Over that ridge, just ahead."

They parked their bikes on top of the ridge and paced down the steep slope another 100 feet, where the sled was waiting.

"We can bring our sled beside this broken one. The three of us can flip it over on top of the other one and tow it back to camp."

"Hey, guys, what is that noise? I hear a rumble," said Crystal.

Then a shock registered on Jon's face. "Stampede!" he shouted.

Jon rushed ahead of them up the slope to the bikes. When Jon jumped on his bike, he was knocked to the ground as an antelope leaped over him. More of the antelopes quickly came over the crest of the hilltop toward them.

"Too late," said Tom. "Run the other way!" Tom shouted.

The antelopes came by the in dozens, hundreds, and then thousands as the creatures rushed past them.

"Try to jump on their back and hang on tight," Tom yelled.

Crystal was the first to jump on the back of an antelope as she wrapped her arms around its thin neck. Tom was hit from behind and fell to the ground. Tom rolled over to one side and then the other to avoid getting trampled by their hoofs. Another antelope tumbled to the ground, and Tom jumped on its back, holding on tightly. The stampede ran for a dozen miles before the herd settled down. Exhausted, they fell off the antelopes to lay on the ground.

Tom woke up, unsure of how long he had slept, and heard Crystal's voice. "Don't move," she whispered in his ear, "or you will start another stampede. How is your head?"

"Sore," Tom replied. Tom looked around to see that they were completely surrounded by the antelopes.

"How long was I out?"

"Not too long, about 30 minutes."

"Have you tried your comlink for help?"

"No, it's broken."

"I'll use mine, then." Tom reached for his pocket notepad, but it was missing. Tom observed the slow-moving antelopes. "At this rate, the last of the antelopes won't pass us until morning."

"Longer if they spend another night here," said Crystal.

Tom nodded his head in agreement. "I think you are right. Some of them are sitting on the ground. If we spend the night here, the dew in the early morning will soak us. At least we will be warm, though. In a few more hours, it will be dark. Look on the bright side; we will have the stars and the two moons for a romantic evening."

"Tom, have you forgotten? The outpost is leaving tomorrow."

"I can guarantee there will be a search party tomorrow. They aren't leaving us behind. Besides, you are their only pilot."

"I hope you're right, but you are wrong about me being the only pilot. Karl was a former pilot for the Navy. He was hiding here because he is facing a court martial for disobeying orders."

"Do you think Jon escaped the stampede?" Crystal asked.

"It's hard to say; Jon was hit quite hard by the antelope. The rescue party will be organized first thing in the morning."

"I hope the rescue party doesn't start another stampede," Crystal said dryly.

"Look," Tom pointed, as the clouded sky was turning red. "It will be dark soon. In another four hours, the clouds will disperse, and we will see the stars. It's going to be a long night for us."

"Not if we spend the night talking. Tell me about your days back at the palace."

Crystal smiled. "It's beautiful."

***

"Have you got any more of those ration bars?"

"None. Nor any water," said Tom.

"Look," Crystal pointed, "There are the bikes," she said as she ran ahead.

When Tom caught up with Crystal, they were stunned by what they saw. The bikes and sled were heavily damaged and surrounded by thousands of small, freshly stripped, clean bones.

"What's going on here?" Crystal asked.

Tom searched the area, then concluded, "It looks like as the antelope came over the crest, one by one, they tripped over the bikes and were trampled by the other antelopes. There must have been over a hundred injured antelopes lying around when the scavengers came by and had a huge feast."

"Crystal, I hate to say this, but..."

"Don't say it; I don't even want to think about it," Crystal said as she sat on the broken bike. "We are 30 miles from the outpost and have no food or water. At any time now, the outpost will be moving halfway around the world." Crystal realized she was talking to herself and was alone. "Tom? TOM!" Crystal shouted.

"I'm over here," said Tom from a distance.

Crystal saw Tom walking back toward the bikes, carrying something in his hands. It was one of the bike's backpacks.

"It's in rough shape, but the food rations and water canteen are okay." Tom removed the canteen from the pack and gave it to Crystal.

"Let's see if we can find the other two packs somewhere."

"I found another one," said Tom. "It's underneath the bike."

"And I found the third pack, but it's been torn to shreds. Look at this," Crystal said as she gave Tom the empty canteen. "The canteen has a line of deep holes—teeth imprints. Something else for us to be concerned about," Crystal said grimly.

"The stunners are nowhere to be seen. Do you want to rest or continue on?" Tom asked.

"I've had enough of looking at these bones. Let's go now," Crystal replied.

***

"Hey, I remember this place. The outpost must be just over the hill," Crystal said as she ran ahead of Tom.

When Crystal suddenly stopped at the crest, she dropped down to her knees. "The campground is empty."

Tom was standing beside her when Crystal burst out, "They think we are dead and left us behind! How pathetic can these guys be? We are not dead!" Crystal screamed. "They are 12,000 miles away from us, Tom! 12,000 miles," Crystal muttered. "What are we going to do now?"

Tom squatted down and held her hand. "The only thing we can do is travel on. We will eat, sleep, and trust in God's direction."

"What does your God have to say, Tom?" Crystal asked bitterly.

Tom released her hand, rose to his feet, and walked a few paces. After a minute of silence, Tom replied, "We go north."

Crystal sighed, stood up, and said, "North is as good as any, I suppose." Crystal paced past Tom as he watched her march ahead. Tom stared at her, then smiled as he ran to catch up with her.

***

"There it is, Crystal. The sanctuary."

At the site of the sanctuary, Crystal could see black slate hoodoos of various sizes. A few small trees filled the gaps between the hoodoos.

"How come we never explored this area?" Crystal asked.

Tom replied, "It's one of the first places where the outpost conducted their research. When we first arrived at the outpost, this place was being explored."

"What do you know about this place?"

"Only what Tony told me. There are quite a few large and small caves in the slate rocks. If we can find the right cave, it will be our shelter. There are trees you can't find anywhere else. There are freshwater springs, and somewhere out there is a hot spring."

"That is all very good, Tom, but what about food? Our rations are almost finished."

"The good news is that Karl said the grains and wildlife are safe to eat. The bad news is we need to kill and consume the flesh."

Crystal, feeling ill, said, "I need to be alone for a minute," as she looked for a place to have some privacy from Tom. After a few minutes of trying to block out the uncomfortable thought of consuming flesh, her stomach started to settle down.

Crystal looked around for a high viewpoint to establish her bearing and saw one that looked promising. Crystal climbed up the steep slope on all fours and finally stopped at the top of the hoodoos. The hoodoos spread out as far as her eyes could see. Crystal whistled for Tom to look up, and he shook his head as he climbed up toward her.

When Tom met up with Crystal, he sat down beside her. "I saw something move, but it was too far away to tell what it was."

"Probably a Rex," said Tom.

"You never told me there are Rexes here," Crystal cried.

"The Rexes are everywhere, and here is no different. Don't forget, Tony said the Rexes have never been known to attack, even here. They are just a little scary to look at."

"Just to show that you have my vote of confidence; you can stand between them and me," said Crystal.

Tom laughed and said, "I'll try to remember that."

"What did Tony make of this place?" Crystal asked.

"It is all mud that was compressed into slate during the ice cap years. When the glacier retreated, the intense weight of the ice created deep erosion in the slate. We should find shelter near a spring before it gets dark."

"There is no shortage of caves around here, and I like this one the best," said Crystal. "The cool water spring nearby makes this cave a good choice, too."

"Something is not right, though, about this cave. It's too clean."

"Why is that an issue?" Crystal inquired.

"I don't know," replied Tom. "Tony told me that the Rexes dug out the caves."

"Then again, we can just be glad that the house cleaning is already done." Crystal smiled. "What we need to do next is to make some bedding."

"It's kind of late for that, as the sun is beyond the horizon now. We can use the backpacks to support our heads against the cave wall."

Crystal sat down near Tom and asked, "Have you ever consumed real flesh?"

Tom replied, "My mother was raised on a domestic animal farm. Synthetic meat was only part of our diet."

"Things were different when I grew up on *Marvel*. My father often ate real meat, but he had to change his diet when my mother married him. It was a big adjustment for Bill."

"Who is Bill?" Tom asked.

"Bill was our chef aboard *Marvel*, and he was also like an uncle to me. Bill was a storyteller as far back as I can remember. Sometimes it wasn't easy for me to be the only child on board. My father and mother were good parents, but it wasn't enough, especially when I was in my teen years. I even began to tune out Sara, the ship computer; she was my best friend."

"Your ship computer had a name?"

"Yes, Sara was not the original ship computer. Father got lucky when he found her in a scrap yard. It turns out Sara was one of the most advanced computers ever designed."

"Where did Sara come from?"

"Father won't tell me or anyone else, except for mother. Father said that some things just couldn't be told. I don't like secrets; it's one of the reasons for my being so ornery. Let's have a truce between us. I won't keep secrets from you, and you don't keep secrets from me. Is that a deal?"

"It's a deal," Tom said, smiling.

"It's pitch black outside. We should call it a night so that we can get up early tomorrow," said Crystal.

"I've got a question for you: I lost my teddy bear; can I sleep beside you?" Tom smiled.

Crystal was trying hard not to laugh, then replied with a soft smile, "You may." Tom and Crystal turned off their torches, and he snuggled beside her.

Late in the night, a large, formless movement from the dim reflection of the planet's two moons gathered outside the cavern, more curious than threatening. They sensed a strange but familiar odour being released from the cavern. They stood together outside the cave entrance, then heard a commotion inside.

Crystal screamed and said, "TOM, WAKE UP! SOMETHING IS CRAWLING OVER ME!"

Tom turned on his torch and was horrified by dozens of green, four-legged spider-like creatures the size of a fist crawling along the cave floor.

"Kill the obnoxious things and throw them out," Crystal demanded.

As Tom stomped the spiders one by one and threw them outside, a dead spider hit a creature in the chest and fell to its feet. The creature realized what it was, quickly picked it up, and ran into the darkness. Another creature took his spot, was rewarded with dead spiders, and also ran off. After Tom killed all the spiders, he lay down on his back, exhausted.

"You missed these two. Never mind, I will handle them," said Crystal as she took them outside and ran into one of the creatures. There was just enough light from the cavern to see the outline of the creature. As Crystal looked up, she was terrified as she was standing face-to-face with a Rex. The Rex, surprised by the near impact, looked down at the dead spiders in Crystal's palm and pointed at her hand.

Crystal stuttered, "You want them? Here, take them both." The Rex took both spiders and disappeared beyond the cavern lights.

When her heart rate settled down, she heard Tom's voice. "Hey Crystal, are you all right?"

"I am now. The Rexes were here, and they took off with all the dead spiders. The spiders must be a delicacy for them. The cavern darkness may have attracted the spiders. We could leave the torch on in the cave, or we could try to follow the Rexes. I don't think they will harm us."

"I doubt we will be able to sleep tonight. Which direction did they go in?" Tom asked.

"The Rexes all went that way," Crystal pointed out.

"I suppose you still want me to lead the way?"

Crystal smiled in the near darkness and said, "How about I hold your hand?"

"An excellent suggestion," Tom replied. The cloudless night sky and the two moons overhead helped them to see the winding trail throughout the hoodoos. "I don't think we are going to find our way back tonight."

"I'm not sure I want to," said Crystal. "There is a light shining ahead. I think it's a campfire."

The trail led to a large open field. In the middle of the field was a circular row of Rexes sitting around a campfire. The open part of the circle faced toward them, and all the Rexes' heads turned in their direction.

"This gives me an eerie feeling; let's go back," Crystal requested.

"We can't," said Tom. "The trail behind us is blocked by the Rexes. We might as well continue toward them."

Tom studied the Rexes' faces and their body language, but nothing registered that could help him understand their motives as he and Crystal entered the circle.

"They are watching us like hawks," said Crystal.

"They are probably studying us, as I am them," said Tom.

"What have you learned so far?"

"Nothing yet," Tom replied.

Two Rexes rose to their feet and stood aside, then moved their hands toward the empty spot.

"I think they want us to sit there," Crystal pointed out. "Their hospitality is a good sign; we should take advantage of this opportunity."

Tom and Crystal sat down between the Rexes as they began to talk among themselves.

"Why are they using their hands so much?" said Crystal.

"It looks like they are using some sort of sign language along with verbal sounds."

Crystal counted the Rexes and said, "Not counting the youngsters, there are fifty adults here in the circle."

All the Rexes stopped communicating when a young Rex carried two small black bowls filled with a white shredded substance and placed them on the ground in front of them.

"What is it?" Crystal asked as Tom reached for the bowl. Tom knew what it was from the smell.

"You don't want to know, but it is cooked well."

"You've got to be kidding," Crystal said in anguish.

"We must not disappoint our hosts." Tom took one of the pieces of white meat and ate it. "This is quite good;

It tastes like sweet crab meat."

"Tom, I don't think I can do this."

"You should if you want to be accepted by the Rexes," Tom said as he ate another piece. Tom removed a canteen and said, "Don't chew on the meat; just quickly swallow it and gulp it down with water."

"You'd better not laugh, or you will surely regret it." Crystal quickly gulped down the water after swallowing the white meat and fought down the urge to throw up.

The Rexes, satisfied, returned to their conversation among themselves.

"I guess we passed the test," said Crystal.

Tom finished the last of the meat and studied the bowl. "Look at this carving. It's very artistic and well done."

"My father was a collector. He would have loved to have this bowl," said Crystal. "I wonder what the carving represents. I saw this black stone before in one of my father's collections from Earth. Black argillite stone. A high-carbon condensed slate that has been heated at a high temperature. I would like to find out more about this artistic bowl; we might learn something."

"While you're doing that, I will brush up on my sign language."

"You know sign language?" Crystal asked doubtfully.

"Yes, because hearing impediments is a thing of the past, it is a lost art. That's why we use sign language among us hackers to avoid eavesdroppers. Let's mingle with the crowd and meet up again later on."

Crystal watched Tom join a trio, studying them to learn their language. The child came back for the bowl, and Crystal decided to follow the young Rexes. The child exited the circle, and Crystal lost sight of the Rexes in the dark. There was no question; the Rexes could see in the dark much better than her. She debated whether she should risk alarming the Rexes with her torch. Crystal turned and was shocked to realize that she was further away from the circle. All she could see behind her was darkness.

Crystal removed her torch and turned it on. She could see that the child, a short distance away, had stepped off the trail to the right and entered the hoodoos. Crystal rushed ahead to catch up with the child. When she arrived at the hoodoos, she was surprised to see several carved doors. She wondered which door the child had entered, but then it exited, answering her question. The child stood still outside the door, fixated by the light in her hand.

Crystal bent down in front of the child and said, "It's okay, see," as she moved the light around. Crystal pointed to the door. "Bowl?" She made a circle in the dirt on the ground, repeated the word, and pointed again at the door. The child took hold of Crystal's hand and brought her inside the hoodoos. The torch revealed shelves of carved bowls and cups, both large and small. Crystal studied the carvings and recorded the images with her implant.

These illustrations on the bowls are all different, Crystal thought. *I wonder what is behind the other doors outside.* When she finished recording the images, she noticed the child was gone.

Crystal left the room and went to enter the other door, but was interrupted by an adult rex, who motioned for her to follow him. Reluctantly, Crystal followed the rex back to the circle. Crystal saw Tom and sat down next to him.

"Did you learn anything, Tom?"

"I recorded 100 signs and stored them in my implant. The Rexes in this circle represent three different tribes. To bypass the language barrier, they use sign language. We are spending the night in one of their chambers tonight, sealed off from the spiders and the Grunts -a predator, as they seem to call it. There are not many Grunts around, but they have a reputation for being extremely quick and can break bones with their jaws. A rat-sized scavenger is responsible for stripping the bones we saw earlier. But they are usually harmless. The Rexes are turning in for the night now," Tom said as he helped Crystal get up.

A group of ten Rexes led them to a cavern with a simple curved door. Tom and Crystal found a spot with a leather mat to lay down.

"This is a big improvement from the last cave," Tom remarked. In the dark, Tom whispered in Crystal's ear,

"I want to tell you something tonight. Thank you for being my best friend."

Crystal, caught off guard, responded by hugging his arm before falling asleep.

Chapter 11

Crystal followed Tom behind a single long column of Rexes carrying spears, poles, ropes, and backpacks on a northward hunting expedition. At the back of the line was Anirudh, the leader of the hunting party. The elder Rexes led the pack, setting the pace for those behind them, with the strongest members in the middle and the leader at the back, as he watched the rear and sometimes guided the caravan. The well-worn soft silt pathway eventually gave way as the trail quickly sank below the ground surface to the exposed slate ground. The submerged trail provided a welcome relief from the constant wind, as the ground surface was well above their heads.

Crystal's memory was jogged by the Holloway trail formation; a historical marvel manifested as trenches carved into the earth. These sunken lanes, also known as Holloways, were not just any old thoroughfares but centuries-old paths that bore witness to the passage of time. The erosion caused by the Rexes' feet, combined with condensed water, was a testament to the historical significance of this trail formation.

The Holloways, even had their ecology, such as the spreading tiny round green-leaved plants that preferred the disturbed earth.

"This trail must be centuries old," Crystal said. "How long is it?" she asked.

Tom replied, "Sixty-five miles. Then, the trail ends at a large valley where our friends will hunt for antelope."

Crystal watched several animals that looked like green mice bury themselves in the tiny, broad-leaved plants that covered the walls of the Holloway.

"Why do all the plants and animals only come in one colour, green?" Crystal asked.

"I asked Ken during one of our assignments together, but he didn't know. It's all genetic-related and not caused by environmental influences, except for the Grunts," Tom replied.

"What are the Grunts?" Crystal asked.

"I asked Ken that same question, but Tony interrupted our conversation when he asked for my assistance. When we see an animal that isn't green, then we will know what a Grunt is," said Tom. "We haven't seen a Grunt since we arrived on Green Shield, so they must be a rarity."

"Have you asked the Rexes about the Grunts?" Crystal asked.

Tom replied, "Yes, but they refused to talk about the Grunts, as they consider them an abomination, so I left the subject alone. The Rexes are confusing and complex creatures. Their characteristics can be silly. They can be laid back for a moment, and then they can become very serious and extremely motivated in their tasks."

"Their art and crafts are very well made. They seem to describe their lifestyle, which doesn't seem to have changed for centuries," said Crystal.

"How do you know their culture hasn't changed?" Tom asked.

"Do you remember the door next to the argillite plates and bowls we found?" Tom nodded his head. "I entered the second door one day and found a huge pile of broken plates and bowls. I quickly searched through the pile, and their artwork was very consistent. One of these days, I'm going to search the pile back at the end of the room," said Crystal.

Crystal felt as if she had lost track of time. When she checked with her implant, she was surprised to learn that eleven hours had gone by since they entered the Holloway. The Rexes took a right turn and walked up a short trail that led out of the trenches and onto an earlier-made campground.

Crystal stopped to look at the endless sea of grass and asked Rex, "Anirudh, why are we stopping here?"

"We will rest here for the night; the trenches will be too damp and wet during the night," Anirudh replied.

Crystal had learned to recognize the Rexes' body language and could tell they were uneasy.

"Is there something wrong?" Crystal asked.

"There is death in the air," said Anirudh as he pointed up to the sky near the eastern horizon. "I will send a senior scout to investigate, along with two trainee hunters and Tom."

Crystal removed the binoculars from her backpack as she focused and could see huge flocks of green, scaly birds circling in the sky. She had learned that Green Shield's birds normally live by themselves, and the presence of a flock indicates that a feast has awakened them. Crystal watched as the Rexes and Tom wandered off and faded away on the distant foothill, a rarity in the vast grassy plain.

The Rexes and Crystal began setting up the camp. The campground was sheltered by mounds of earth for protection from the relentless wind. A large, circular patch of ground raised in the middle for sleeping was quickly layered with green fur-covered hides. Crystal spread out her mat and sat down.

One hour later, Crystal watched as the dimming glow of the sun from the west, which usually failed to penetrate through the clouds, vanished below the western horizon. A mixture of dried grass and dung was piled up in the middle of the campsite and set alight. Anirudh sat down beside Crystal, and they communicated through sign language.

"We received light messages from the distant hillside.[2] They have found something of interest and will investigate it in the morning, as it's too late to come back tonight." For a long moment, Anirudh stared into the distance, then made a low clicking sound.

Crystal knew he was upset and asked, "What is wrong?"

"The messages have stopped without the usual closing words," Anirudh replied and added, "In the morning, we will take up arms and investigate it. The search party may need our help."

Crystal's sudden fear for Tom's safety weighed heavily on her mind. *Oh God, please look out for Tom. He is all I have in this world.* At that moment, Crystal was shocked by who she had asked but quickly dismissed it from her mind. *It must be Shelia's memory that has influenced me, or was it my mother during my childhood years? Within an hour, the clouds will disperse, and the stars will shine throughout the night.* Crystal sat on her makeshift bed, and for the first time, she felt very alone.

Crystal and the remaining Rexes gathered in a tight circle near the dimming dung fire. She felt so small in merging with them, but she also felt protected from the night predators that may have been lurking nearby. By now, she was able to grasp their spoken language. The tone of their voice indicated disgust as she listened to their conversation. The "abominations" had been sighted nearby.

---

[2] *The Rexes send messages by reflecting light off mirrors to communicate over a great distance.*

Crystal knew they were talking about the Grunts. Unlike all the other living animals and plant life, the Grunts were a mix of red and white, not green. Tom and Crystal were never able to understand their displeasure with the Grunts, as they had always walked away when asked.

The heavy clouds soon disappeared, and the stars gradually filled the darkening sky. Already, the ground was soaked from the dewdrops as the Rexes began their conversation, which revealed a story about each star. Anirudh asked, "Which star do your people come from?"

Crystal was caught off guard, as they had never asked this before, and replied, "My people are spread out among 65 different stars, but the world I was born in revolved around that star near the horizon," And she added, "Why haven't you asked me this before?"

"I was ashamed to ask," said Anirudh.

Crystal, surprised, asked. "I don't understand; why would you be ashamed?"

"It's not me, it's all of us," said Anirudh. "It's all explained by the plates."

Crystal, puzzled, said, "You are referring to the pattern on the black slate plates and bowls," as she became excited by this new revelation.

Anirudh wrapped his arms around himself and said, "I talk too much," and added, "This is too painful to continue."

"But why?" Crystal asked. "Every time Tom and I ask about the symbols on the plates, your people walk away."

"The symbols remind us of how our master rejected us and left us behind," said Anirudh.

"Where are your masters?" Crystal asked.

Anirudh replied. "They returned to their world after they fought with the abomination."

"You mean the Grunts?" Crystal asked.

"No, the abomination used the Grunts as hunters against us, as we failed to protect our masters," Anirudh replied.

Crystal was quiet as she absorbed the Rexes' history and asked, "How long ago did this happen?"

"Long ago. Beyond countless years," Anirudh replied.

"Anirudh, why do your people call your master's rivals 'the abomination'?"

Anirudh thought for a moment to find the right word and said, "They were not real."

***

Early the next morning, Tom was sleeping on his back under the blanket, and he awoke to foul air. Tom realized it was coming from the breath of a red and white-speckled short-haired Grunt inches from his face. Tom suddenly became alert when the Grunt displayed its teeth. The Grunt didn't attack and instead only looked curious. Then, Tom was shocked when the Grunt sat on its rear end and used its front limbs to ask in sign language, "Are you their master?"

The muffled noise from Tom's blanket woke up one of the Rexes, who saw the Grunt as he rose to his feet. The Grunt, alarmed, ran off toward the black shale terrain with a series of short cries. Tom was amazed by the Grunt's speed as it disappeared beyond the boulders. Diya was the first to offer her apologies and ask forgiveness, as she had failed to notice the Grunt.

Tom, surprised by Diya's humbleness, said, "It's all right. No one was hurt."

Diya, relieved, said. "It will not happen again. It was a juvenile. An adult would not have hesitated to attack you."

Tom nodded his head as he remembered how fast the Grunt could run and said, "He tried to communicate with me."

Diya, visibly upset as shown by the quick motion of her sign language, replied, "We are not to speak of the matter again," and moved away.

Tom, puzzled by Diya's reaction and the Grunt's intelligence, gathered up his blanket and belongings and strapped them to his backpack. He followed the Rexes toward the base of a stony foothill. There was a sudden commotion among the Rexes, as they appeared aggravated while making clicking sounds. Tom asked Diya, "Why are you angry? What is wrong?"

Diya replied, "Ayaka, our senior scout and messenger have disappeared. He didn't return to camp this morning. I sent a hunter up to the summit, where he was last seen. Without Ayaka, there is no one else who can use the mirror to communicate back to the main camp." Diya paused for a moment and added, "The Grunt must have taken him by surprise, as he was an almighty hunter and fought many Grunts in the past."

Tom watched as they removed their grass-braided vests and sleeves for protection from their backpacks. Without his sidearm, Tom felt insecure, as he always had to rely on the Rexes for protection. They took stock of their bows and arrows with the embedded, sharp-edged glass arrowheads. After witnessing the young Grunt's amazing swiftness, he realized that the Rexes' real advantage was their immense strength. Tom knew the Rexes wouldn't retreat to the main camp, as their philosophy was to fight to the last as a way to pay tribute to their unknown and long-gone master.

Tom heard a Rex rush over from a nearby hill and stood before Diya. Tom listened as the scout said, "Ayaka is missing, but we found his mirror on the ground, and the area is covered with scavengers. I don't know what they are feeding on, as no bones are lying nearby, but Ayaka's clothes are scattered among the scavengers." The Rexes expressed their anger by making clicking noises.

Tom had seen a colony of scavengers, rat-sized green animals that could strip clean the flesh from bone in minutes. They were usually harmless but could sense a dead animal from a long distance away with their powerful noses. He had an uncomfortable feeling about this and asked, "Show me this, as I would like to see it for myself."

When they arrived at the site, Tom bent down on one knee as the animals scattered away. As he examined closer, his worst fear was verified. *A G-Gun was used here!* The Genocide Systematic Cellular Destruction Gun, the most fearful weapon known, which caused the body's cells to separate from the bio-glue that holds them together. Being found in possession of such a weapon warrants execution by the Commonwealth authorities. Tom considered that the Thracian might be nearby but found this unlikely because their home-world empire was more than 70 light-years away and beyond the Borderland.

Tom rose to his feet and said, "Diya, I believe Ayaka's body is what the scavenger was feeding on. Another off-world alien may be responsible for Ayaka's death, and there may be others still nearby that may endanger our lives. Your armour vest will not protect you from their weapon, as it causes your entire body to explode. You will have to use your wits if you want to win this battle."

Diya stood silently for several moments before going to talk with the other Rexes. She turned away and asked Tom,

"Will you combine your wisdom with ours to defeat this off-world enemy?"

"Yes, but I can't promise we will be successful," replied Tom.

"We will find this criminal and plan a strategy to fight them," said Diya. "For now, we will go east, then north, where the Grunt stronghold is located, which is close to the great sand border. It is only a short day's walk from here," said Diya.

***

The early morning daylight stirred Crystal from her sleep when she heard Anirudh say, "It's time."

Crystal was surprised to see that the Rexes had outfitted themselves in their combat grass-entwined vests and were holding weapons without her being aware. *They are very quiet*, thought Crystal. *No wonder the Rexes could sneak up close to an antelope.* Crystal hurried to gather her bedroll and gear into her backpack. Crystal walked to the rear with Anirudh as the Rexes followed the beaten path made the day before by the first pursuers. Crystal asked Anirudh, "Do you know what is ahead of us?"

Anirudh replied, "Beyond the grassy plain lie the rock mounds, and further north is a valley where there is a Grunt holdout. Beyond that is the great sandy desert that extends north and then expands west and east. In the valley, there may be much death."

"Do you think something has happened to the Grunts?" Crystal asked.

"No, but it would please us if something did and would give us peace in our souls," Anirudh replied.

***

With the late sun behind them, the Rexes steadily crawled up to the top of the high hill crest, overlooking the valley below. As they spread out along the crest, Diya motioned to Tom to come and see for himself. Tom and the Rexes were shocked by the destruction and the many dead Grunts. The smell of rotting corpses and smoke filled the air as the warm, dry breeze moved up the hillside. Tom observed the oblong valley from north to south. A small lake to the left seemed to be fed by a small spring on the opposite hill. On this side of the lake was a large aquaculture plot. Tom perceived that the Grunts were either herbivores or omnivores, unlike the Rexes, who were carnivores. Near the south end of the lake, a large open canopy is attached to a small grey building and a tower. *Or perhaps a water tower?* Tom thought. Within the canopy, there was an object, but it was too far to tell its purpose as there were no roads nearby. Tom could see hundreds of small grey pillbox buildings, and the Grunts entered or emerged from this shelter. Tom understood that the Grunts were below-ground dwellers, and the semi-transparent glass tops must be their sources of light below ground. To the far right of the valley, Tom was shocked to see that a mass of white objects was Grunt skeletons that had been thrown into piles.

Tom spotted the first evidence of off-world aliens' presence: a group of six streaks of blackened exhaust on the open ground. Tom asked his subconscious memory what fit the exhaust pattern, and he received the answer: a Thracian military craft, possibly a carrier for 20 soldiers. *What reason would the Thracian have for being here?* Tom thought, as there was nothing he could see that would interest them and leave behind such destruction. This was the first time he had observed the physical nature of the Grunts. *They walk like biped but run on all four limbs. And they are fast,* Tom thought, truly impressed.

Tom's thoughts were interrupted when Diya said, "The Grunts have spotted us."

"Where are they?" Tom asked. "I don't see any unusual activities down below."

"They are behind us," Diya replied.

Tom turned around, and from a short distance, he could see over one hundred angry Grunts. Tom groaned and quietly said,

"This isn't going very well for us. The Grunts outnumber us nearly 30 to one."

***

Crystal, tired from the journey and her back aching from carrying the backpack, heard Anirudh say, "I smell death."

Crystal, now alert, observed the surroundings. The green grassland ended a short distance behind them as they entered a rough, black-grey shale terrain. The trail led to an empty campground, which the Rexes searched along with the outlying areas. Anirudh picked small pieces of grass fibres off the ground.

Crystal asked, "What did you find?"

"The search party senses danger and has put on their amour."

One of the Rexes came down from the hilltop and said, "I found the source of death but found nobody and no signs of corpses being carried away. This is very strange."

Crystal's fear for Tom's life made her more determined to press on, and she asked, "Anirudh, which way did they go?"

Anirudh pointed toward the east. Without another word, Crystal immediately took the path Anirudh had pointed out.

***

It was noon the next day when the Grunts led Tom and the Rexes from the underground pillbox with their arms bound together. Tom, trying to feel positive about their ordeal, said to Diya, "The Grunts didn't kill us or harm us, which, as you said, is against their nature. And they haven't eaten us either."

"That's because they are vegetarians," Diya replied.

Tom was surprised to learn about this considering their history of violent attacks toward the Rexes. *So why are we still alive?* Tom thought as he saw a Grunt carrying another pile of bones, realizing that the bones were those of other Grunts.

"Diya, all those piles of bones we saw are Grunts."

Diya replied in agreement, "The bones were fresh, which means the scavengers have had a feast for the last few days. Perhaps the off-world creatures you mentioned last night are responsible for the killing. But why were the bones remaining when those of our scout were not?"

Tom replied, "They have different types of weapons that can injure or kill." Tom heard a commotion among the Grunts, and one broke away and walked toward Tom, stopping a few feet away. Using sign language, he said, "You and your slaves will follow us." Diya and the others signalled through their clicks that they were angry about being called slaves.

Tom ignored his friends and replied, "Lead the way." The Grunts formed a circle around Tom and the Rexes as they walked toward the lake.

The Grunts may have assumed that my off-world appearance means that I am the Rexes' leader or master. Tom thought. As he walked closer to the large canopy, the young and old joined the crowd, as they emerged from their underground dwellings.

Crystal discreetly watched from the hillcrest; it was a relief to see Tom and the others alive. "How are we going to rescue them when there are so many Grunts?" Crystal asked.

"That isn't the only question," Anirudh replied. "Why are they still alive and being led toward the large canopy near the lake?"

Crystal took her binoculars out of her backpack and focused on the canopy. She zoomed in on the building and saw a wheeled cart that could hold a dozen seats and a deck. The cart was on a parallel track that travelled below ground, and there was a stairway beside the tracks. *The Grunts are much more intelligent than I thought. They are probably taking them deep underground.*

When they all entered beneath the canopy, Tom could see the object was an open 12-seat cart on tracks with a thick cable that led down below ground. Another set of tracks parallel to the cart stood empty. Tom looked closer at the cart and saw that the lower floor and the building all consisted of rough grey glass. Surprised, Tom noticed that everything in this structure was made of glass. Tom took his ring and tried to scratch the glass. When it wasn't able to, he guessed that it was phiale glass, a form of break-resistant glass.

The cart had a large tank on the front and rear ends of the cart and a cargo area in the middle. From the stubby ground tower, the Grunts began filling the cart with water. Then, Tom realized what he saw: the entire system was a funicular railway. As one car went up the tunnel, it was balanced by a car on the other side, attached via a cable, which went down. Huge water tanks made the descending car heavy enough to be able to pull up the ascending car. The glass wire along the top of the tunnel used a telegraph that allowed the conductor of the car at the bottom to tell the workers at the top how many passengers he had and, therefore, how much water had to be added to the opposite car. The ascending and descending vehicles counterbalanced each other to move both passengers and cargo.

When the tank was filled, a Grunt told Tom and his friends to sit in the cart's seat. The cart moved toward the entrance and disappeared below the ground. Soon after, the last of the Grunts, including the maintenance workers, disappeared below ground.

The Grunts continued down below along the descending walkway.

Crystal watched as Tom moved out of sight and lowered her binoculars. She turned to Anirudh and said, "It seems the entire township has gone below ground. We may be able to follow them without being noticed."

Anirudh agreed, spoke with his colleague, and replied, "Let us get started," as they quickly sprinted down the slope toward the canopy.

When Tom's eyes adjusted to the ceiling's narrow line of dim lights, he could see that the tunnel wall was lined with a vertical ribbed glass structure as the cart travelled downward. *This tunnel and the glass components seem beyond the Grunts' capabilities. Perhaps the answers will be found at the end of the ride. The cart and the tunnel are clean, so the Grunts must keep everything maintained and in order.*

When the cart arrived at the bottom of the slope and stopped, Tom got out. He was led to another tunnel and walkway that went another couple hundred feet and opened into a large open room supported by pillars. Like the tunnel, everything was lined with the same ribbed glass, only this time the pillars were the light sources. The room was huge, as there was more than enough room for the Grunts. In the middle of the room was a large, overturned bowl with a flat platform above it that seemed to be made of ceramic. The structure had a circular beam over the top of it. Nearby was what appeared to be a large stack of black crystal plates that seemed to fit the empty slots around the bowl.

Shortly after, a crowd of Grunts filled the cave. Tom noted that many of the injured were supported by others or on crutches. An elderly Grunt broke free from the crowd, approached Tom, and said, "I am Tiff," then paused to examine Tom. "You are not like the others who invaded us and harmed many of our people. Are you the Rexes' master from the ancient days?"

Tom replied, "No, I don't know who their master was, as I am an off-world visitor. My friend and I met the Rexes six months ago and have lived among them."

Tiff became visibly upset and turned to walk back to his group of elders as they discussed their dilemma. Moments later, they came back and said, "It has been determined; you will deceive us like the others off-world and must be put to death."

"Why?" Tom asked, "We have done nothing wrong. Who are the others you are talking about?"

Tiff replied, "They called themselves the 'Thracian' and tried to take our crystal plates away. We thought they were our God that who come back to us, but they lied. When they tried to take away the crystal, we resisted, and they killed our spiritual elder. We fought back, but many of us were killed or wounded. They are mighty warriors. They are strong like the Rexes and quick, but we were faster."

Tom couldn't argue with that, as he had seen how fast the Grunts could move on all four limbs.

Tiff continued, "Their weapons were powerful. Many of us were killed, and others were burned. They retreated up to the surface and escaped in their flying craft. Now you are here to steal the crystal, too?"

"No, we are here to investigate why one of our scouts died, and now we believe the Thracians are responsible," Tom replied.

"Only one?" The elder said and continued "Twenty-five, of us died, and many more were injured!"

"Were any of the Thracians killed? Tom asked.

Tiff replied, "No, but many are injured, and we seized two of their weapons!" as he displayed his teeth in satisfaction.

"Since we know the truth, we will return to our camp base and continue on our journey," said Tom.

"No!" said the elder, "You may go, but the Rexes will die!"

"Why?" Tom asked, "They are my friends and have done nothing wrong."

"They are an abomination and must die!" the elder said.

Tom was shocked by Tiff's outburst but remembered that the Rexes had said the same thing about the Grunts.

Another Grunt approached the elder and whispered in his ear. Appearing stunned, Tiff looked at the other villager nearby, sighed, and then nodded his head once in agreement. The elder turned to Tom and said, "If you are truly an off-worlder, then you will have the knowledge to put back the crystal plates in the right order, as the Thracian knew how to disassemble the crystal. If you are successful, then you and your friends may leave unharmed."

Realizing they may have a way out of their predicament, Tom replied, "Okay!" They removed the glass twine from his wrists and stepped aside as Tom walked to the stack of crystal and picked up the top layer. He scrutinized it closely and saw that the patterns were similar to the Rexes' argillite plates. Tom picked up the other plates, as they were all the same size, though the patterns were different. Then he made a shocking discovery. These were quasi-crystals. Like his implants, they were <u>supramolecular aggregates</u> exhibiting both <u>crystalline</u> (solid) properties as well as amorphous, <u>liquid-like</u> properties. They were extremely high-tech.

There was a shout, and the entire crowd turned toward the tunnel. Tom could see that Crystal and the Rexes had made a battle formation with their spears. Tom took advantage of the distraction and seized the glass knife from Tiff and held it at his throat. Tom intensely stared into Tiff's eyes and shook his head from side to side. He hoped Tiff would understand that his people were not to attack and keep the agreement that Tom would place the crystals back in their proper enclosure.

Tiff didn't need to be told what would happen if he decided against Tom's demands. The elder commanded not to attack as Crystal and the others made their way toward Tom.

"I thought for a moment we were done for," said Crystal.

Tom nodded and released the elder. "Tiff, this is my friend. Crystal will help me with the plates."

The elder stared at Crystal and asked, "Why?"

Tom struggled to explain in a way the elder could understand and replied, "She has a gift for reading inside the plates."

The elder's eyes perked up, and he said, "Only the ancient one had the gift to do that!"

"Crystal is another one," Tom insisted.

"Then there is hope," the elder said. "Begin!" he demanded.

Not sure what Tiff meant by this, Tom took Crystal's hand and led her to the plates. "What gifts?" Crystal whispered in Tom's ear.

"Engage your implant and tell me what you register," Tom said as he handed her one of the plates.

Crystal examined the plates and, astonished, looked at Tom. "It's alive!" Crystal picked up another plate and said, "It's alive, too! But how is this possible?" she asked.

Tom replied, "Between my implant and my subconscious mind, I was asked to analyze and communicate with the individual plates. Crystal, they must be destroyed, and I promised the Grunts I would put them back in service."

"But they are alive," said Crystal.

"No, they are not. The plates are only a channel, like a door to another, mind, spirit, or something else. They demanded that I obey their directive. I don't think their purpose is good."

Crystal, more confused than comprehending the situation, asked, "So what should we do?"

Tom replied, "We'll do what I agreed to do while I think of something else," and added, "There seems to be a pattern overlay on each plate, but they don't match the symbols above each slot."

Crystal walked toward the main assembly and asked, "What is this thing?"

"I don't know for sure, but it seems to have multiple functions. One thing I recognize is that the platform is a holographic device, yet the overhead ring seems to be an add-on, as it isn't needed for the hologram."

"Why are the plates to be fitted into the slots? And why was this device installed below ground?" Crystal asked. "You said the plates are dead, not alive. What do you mean by that?"

"Remember when that doctor gave you the false memory of your dead friend, Shelia? Well, I think there is a similarity here. These plates have embedded their memory bank, but they are in stasis, so what would happen if we placed them back in the right slot?"

Crystal held one plate in her left hand and walked counter-clockwise around the structure, sliding her right hand along the surface. She felt a buzz on her hand and static from her implant and cried out to Tom, "I found something." Tom rushed over to Crystal as she said, "Place your hand over this imprint."

Tom touched the symbol but felt nothing.

"Here, let's try this again," she said as she hovered her hand above the symbol and nodded. "It wasn't meant to be touched but hovered over. It's connected with my implant, but it's all garbled." Then Crystal thought she knew the answer. "Tom, this specific plate needs to be connected with each device so that it can be engaged!"

Tom replied, "You may be right. Then we should scrutinize each plate," as he spread out the plates evenly on the glass floor. "Oh, this plate is interesting. This plate has standard data media, and I can interpret it. Crystal, continue installing the plates so that I won't be distracted as I read the data."

Crystal inserted the plates into each slot while Tom studied the data. When Crystal came to the last empty slot, Tom let out a large sigh. "Now I know the truth," said Tom, as he walked up to Crystal.

"What truth?" Crystal asked.

Tom wasn't sure if he should reveal what he learned, but then he remembered his promise to her about not keeping secrets from her. "I was right. We have to destroy this device, and if the Commonwealth ever finds out about it, it will cause havoc in the Five Sectors. We will risk having our minds wiped for certain because we know too much."

Before Tom could explain why, the elder interrupted and asked, "Is this the last plate to insert?"

"Yes," Tom replied as he inserted the last piece and stood back. "I hope this works," Tom whispered to Crystal.

"What did you do?" Crystal asked.

"Remember when I asked back at the forest, 'Do you want the truth or the fake news?'" Crystal nodded her head. "These people have lived with fake news for thousands of years. Now, we will all know the truth about what happened. I used my implant to modify the plates' media instructions. Now watch what is about to happen."

All 22 plates lit up as the inverted bowl formed a hologram image above the platform. A large spaceship was orbiting the planet in an area where the daylight was completely covered by clouds. Tom knew it was Green Shield many years ago-2455 years to be exact. A symbol appeared above the hologram. Tom whispered in Crystal's ears the date. Various flitters left the mother ship and flew down to the planet surface. The view of the planet's was a patch of grey or black shale surrounded by mud because there wasn't any form of life. The lifeless ocean was evenly spread out on the planet.

Tom whispered, "Let's slowly step back near the tunnel exit because the Rexes and the Grunts are going to be angry when they learn the same truth I just found out."

After the flitters landed, many strange machines appeared that Crystal had never seen before. Many of the machines were a smooth, nearly formless light tan with a thin dark stripe. Brown-coloured drones and automated bipeds went about their business, taking soil samples and mapping the terrain. After several months went by, the machines returned to space. The date returned, and Tom told Crystal, "Five years later." A dozen huge ships returned as hundreds of flitters exited the ship and flew down to the planet surface. The flitters hovered near the planet surface, and the hull opened as huge clouds of particles spread out above the planet surface. Crystal realized what they were doing: "They are terraforming the planet," she cried out to Tom. He nodded in return. More ships arrived to continue the operation, then returned to their home bases.

"Where is their home base?" Crystal asked.

"Somewhere beyond the fifth Commonwealth territory," Tom replied.

As the years passed, the planet turned green in the plains, and the trees in the southern and northern hemispheres took root. Years went by before another mothership returned only this time, the ship landed on the green planet.

Tom and Crystal made their way back near the exit. They heard a commotion among the crowd. Crystal looked at the hologram and saw the ships landing on the rocky plain and two different suits of armour exiting the craft, along with many thousands of animals being herded out of the craft. The aliens finally removed their helmets and then suits, then the uproar started. The beings were both the Rexes and the Grunts! The youngsters soon exited the ship, and both the Rexes and the Grunts were playing together as the adults watched on. It was obvious that there was a mutual friendship and cooperative existence between the two groups. Crystal could hear the rumbles and clicks from the natives, who were disturbed by the images. The mothership was their home base. Then, many years later, another ship arrived. The ships were huge, symmetrical shapes made of semitransparent, multi-coloured glass that resembled an ice crystal in appearance.

Crystal seized Tom's arm. "I saw a video before in my grandfather's den," she cried in a low voice. "My parents found a much smaller ancient Warcraft that crashed on a planet in the borderland where my mother died."

The Warcraft suddenly separated into five individual units, and four flew away around the planet. The remaining craft attacked the mothership with a series of orange-pulsing beams. The mothership's force shield absorbed the enemy's beams, but the force field showed signs of weakening, and the evacuation was ordered as hundreds of Rexes and Grunts escaped on the ground or into the atmosphere as the mothership fought back with its weapons. Then it happened— the mothership exploded in a blinding light, leaving behind scorched ground as the ship evaporated into a huge cloud of plasma ionized gas.

"That explains why there wasn't any trace of metal wreckage for the survey team to detect," said Tom.

Later, the other warships returned, reconnected, and landed in the same valley near the lake. A strange glass-like machine exited the ship, began boring into the surface rock and quickly disappeared. The rocks, were vaporized into plasma as the gas rushed out of the tunnel with a hurricane-force wind. Later in the day, the boring machine exited through the second tunnel and stood motionless. The machine transformed into another machine, scooped up the deposit of sand nearby, and began coating the tunnel surface with the grey phiale glass as it moved underground. After the glass construction was completed, along with the cable, the cart, and the water tower, the machine returned to the ship.

"Why were the low-tech cart and tower left behind?" Crystal asked.

"You will see in a minute. The real scary part is about to begin," Tom replied. Another machine exited the warship. This time the machine had legs, and it entered the tunnel as the warship rose and returned off-world. "I think a section of the warship might be the one that your parents found," said Tom.

The images shifted as the biped machine entered the middle of the cavern, settled down on the floor, and transformed one last time into the inverted bowl. The hologram was turned on, and an image appeared and he stepped into the room. "It is a transport portal!" Crystal cried. It was a living being, or it seemed like, one as it was nearly as tall as the Rexes, a humanoid, silver-white biped with a slim build and four limbs. *It is quite attractive*, Crystal thought.

"Yes," Tom replied and added, "A transportation device. The glass coating provides a shield from the electronic interference that would disrupt the portal. They chose this planet because most of its heavy minerals that would interfere with the portal are deep underground. And the alien you see is not a living being but a living robot."

"A cyborg?" Crystal asked.

"No," Tom replied. "A cyborg is part machine, part living organism. This robot is designed to be possessed. An avatar."

Crystal, confused, watched as the alien, or machine, walked back to the portal, activated it, and stood back. A flash hit the robot from behind as it flew, crashed into the portal and was motionless. The robot and part of the portal took the brunt of the force. The Rexes and the Grunts appeared with their weapons as they entered the cave. Satisfied that it was safe, the rest of them joined in and embraced each other, unaware of the slight movement of the injured robot. The sudden movement of the alien was astonishingly quick as it rose from the portal and killed or maimed the assailants. When the robot had secured the area, it examined the portal for damage, then went into a rage. Tom whispered, "The portal couldn't be fixed. Therefore, he or she was trapped on this planet all alone and wanted revenge." Tom and Crystal watched how, over time, the robot captured the young Rexes and Grunts and organized hunting parties against each other for many years.

There was an uproar as the natives rushed forward and tried to destroy the portal piece by piece.

"It's time to leave," said Tom. Crystal nodded in agreement and ran up the tunnel with Tom close behind her. When they were back on the surface, Crystal asked, "Whatever happened to the robot?"

"Unlike the robot we encountered south in the forest somewhere on this planet, its power source probably ran out several thousand years ago."

"And over all these years, they have hated and hunted each other," Crystal said quietly. "What do you suppose will happen next?" Crystal asked.

"Do you still have your binoculars with you?" Tom asked.

"I left them behind in my backpack," Crystal replied.

"Good, let's hike back up over the hill, pick up the backpack, and spend the night there. Maybe by morning, they will have settled down and reasoned things out among themselves," said Tom.

***

Tom looked down on the Grunts' townsite with the binoculars, then handed them back to Crystal and said, "Nothing seems to be moving down there on the surface. Except for the children. All the adults are still underground."

"I hope our friends are okay," she said, as she was concerned for Anirudh. "If we don't hear from them by morning, we should head back home."

"We should spend the night over there under that overhead ledge," Tom suggested. Crystal nodded and removed the blanket and padded mat from the backpack.

It was late at night as the stars appeared when Crystal asked under the blanket she shared with Tom. "What did you mean when you said the robot was possessed?"

"When we encountered that robot in the forest, I was puzzled by what he said just before he died. He said, 'Now I return to where I belong.' When I examined the plates in the cave, the one plate that was damaged caused all the other plates to go off-line or to go in static. When all 22 minds joined together, some cosmological constant-pi energy formations were created that opened the portal between this world and their home-world."

"And where is their home world?" Crystal asked.

"I don't know," Tom replied. "But if we ever get off-world, we can't let the Commonwealth know about this," said Tom.

"Why? It's important for the Commonwealth to know about this."

"I agree," said Tom. "But in my years as a cryptologic technician, I found strange actions from the authorities where they removed citizens for asking the wrong questions. I believe that if we report this to the authorities, they will arrange to have our minds wiped because if the public ever finds out, there may be a huge panic, as we only barely won the war during the Robot Revolution 100 years ago. Humanity lost nearly 50 percent of its population during the war. Even worse, you and I know the truth about the robots."

"We do? What is the truth?" Crystal asked.

Tom sighed, "When I said the robots are possessed, I meant to say that they have been taken over by an essential being or a non-body spirit. Probably from Hell, as their intentions are evil."

"Could a cyborg become possessed, too?" Crystal asked?

"I think Bert and I may have run into some already, which included Genet," Tom replied.

Crystal shivered and held Tom tightly. She said, "We're darned if we do or darned if we don't tell the Commonwealth authorities."

"Unfortunately, it's true," said Tom.

***

It was early morning when Crystal poked her head out from under the blanket and saw hundreds of Grunts and a dozen of her friends a short distance away, quietly, patiently waiting. Crystal said softly, "Tom, we have company!"

Tom slowly sat up and stared at the crowd. He said, "They don't seem angry."

Anirudh and the rest of his people walked toward them and sat down. "Fear not. All is well with our renewed friends and us. You and Tom destroyed the great lie that we all believed for untold years. We honour you both for revealing the truth, and we will now confirm with us all that live in our world."

"You will have a big job ahead to convince everyone," said Crystal. Anirudh understood the human gesture and nodded his head. "Anirudh, please ask Tiff to come here." Anirudh got back on his feet and motioned for the elder to come forward.

Tom spoke with his hand and asked Tiff, "In which direction did the Thracian fly away?"

The elder said, "Our people from the east said their sky ship is located a half-day's travel away."

Tom turned to Crystal and said, "I think this might be our way off-world."

Crystal's eyes opened wide, and she said, "Dare we try?"

Chapter 12

The year 2395

Crystal crawled through the tall grass with Tom, as they looked over the valley facing north.

"There's a Thracian warship over a mile away in the valley. What are the Thracians doing here?" Crystal whispered.

Tom gave the binoculars to her and said, "Back at Midway, there was some talk about some Thracian holdouts after the war was over. I guess these Thracians are the renegades. Focus the binoculars to the left of the ship. Those are our people with the blue prison collars around their necks."

"Perhaps they are prisoners of war?"

"That's my guess, too, but perhaps the war efforts haven't worked out for them. The ship is several miles away. There is no way we can get close to the ship to free those people without being noticed."

We may not know a way, but perhaps the Rexes will... Crystal thought.

***

"Commander, we have a visitor. The image is on the forward screen," said the Thracian communication officer. A short, green-haired biped approached the right side of the ship. "It appears to be carrying several large bags supported by straps around its neck."

"Scan it," said the commander.

"The scanner shows no weapons, just some stone objects or artifacts; perhaps some gems."

"Just a trader. We have no use for it. Send the creature away."

"Sir, you might want to look at the gems the scanner is showing."

The commander studied the bag's contents.

"Sir, if there is more of this, it will enhance our status."

"Indeed, it would. I've never seen a black diamond this big before. See what it is willing to trade for it. If it doesn't cooperate, kill it," the commander ordered.

On the other side of the ship, six human prisoners with blue collars around their necks sat on the ground, being watched over by several guardsmen. Two stunners silently fired simultaneously, and the guardsmen fell to the ground. Ten Rexes emerged, grabbed the prisoners and hauled them off into the grass.

"Commander, I have just detected two stunner emissions. One of our sentries is down, and the prisoners have escaped."

The commander watched the Rexes carrying the prisoners and was astonished, as in seconds they disappeared over the hill crest.

"Execute that trader," the commander ordered.

"We cannot, the trader is gone, too. But we have two new prisoners."

"Secure the area, I will see to those two myself."

Crystal couldn't believe how quickly the guard recovered from the impact of their two stunners. *Tom took a direct hit from the guard's stunner, but why did they spare me?* she thought.

A Thracian ensign held onto Crystal's arm. The guardsman walked over to Tom and drew from his holster the most fearful weapon ever known: A G-gun! A horrifying scream escaped Crystal as she kicked the Thracian in the kneecap and broke free from his grip. She ran to lay down on top of Tom to protect him from the G-Gun. Not that it would do any good, for they would both face total bodily destruction. Crystal held Tom tightly, waiting for certain death to come.

When the commander arrived, he asked the guard, "Why the delay?"

"It's the Woman's intervention, sir."

The commander looked down at Crystal and said, "Why would you shield him? He is not worthy of mercy."

"If he is worthy, then it would not be mercy. I will take his place," Crystal replied defiantly.

"Women," the commander said. "It is our custom for you to identify yourself if you wish to take his place."

Crystal slowly rose to her feet, faced the commander and replied. "For the first time in my life, I finally understand my mother. CRYSTAL STYLER IS MY NAME!"

The commander was speechless, and then asked, "And who is your father?"

Crystal replied, "CAPTAIN MARK STYLER OF THE SHIP *MARVEL!*"

The commander sighed and said, "So this is how it will all end."

The commander ordered all his crewmen to return to the ship to prepare to leave. When they were alone, the commander removed his pulse laser handgun, set it on the ground and sat a short distance away.

Crystal, confused by the change of events, asked, "I don't understand, why are you doing this?"

"Because of my oath to your father."

"You knew my father? But I still don't understand."

"Sit down on the other side of my weapon, and I will explain."

***

The year 2388: Two years after Katherine died, four years before Captain Mark and his ship, *Marvel*, went missing, and seven years before the present.

Bridge sector of the ship *Marvel*.

"Mark, please reconsider the options I suggested. We both know these Thracians are bigger, stronger, and faster than any human. Your chances of winning are only 20 percent," said Sara, the ship computer.

"That's why I chose this planet. Besides, I have to get this out of my system. Nothing else works for me. Ever since Kate's death, a piece of me has slowly died every day. I need to get this behind me so that I can get on with my life."

"And what about me and the rest of us, should you lose?"

"I am sorry, Sara, but what do you want of me? The Mark you have known all these years or an empty shell of a man."

Sara sighed, "Or a dead one. Just remember, we all care for you."

"Except for Crystal," Mark whispered.

"Mark, someday she will learn the hard way and come around again."

"Perhaps," said Mark.

"I have detected a Thracian ship's arrival; it is on schedule."

A small Thracian warship landed a short distance from *Marvel* and shut down its engine, as it waited to cool down. The Thracian warship's ramp dropped to the ground as a single Thracian stood at the opening, waiting for the *Marvel's* scanner.

"Identification confirmed. No weapons or body armour. He is your man," Sara announced.

"Good. Now it's my turn. Wish me luck," Mark said, as he exited the side door and waited to be scanned. *Let's hope the thin air and light gravity of this planet will work in my favour*, Mark thought.

Mark and the Thracian walked toward the circle of stones he had set up earlier, and eventually, they were surrounded by large waist-high boulders between the two ships. When the contestants entered the circle, Mark spoke out loud in the Thracian language. "I, Captain Mark Styler, challenge to a duel Commander Casingat of the Langat Klan for the death of my wife, Katherine Styler. Do you accept this duel?"

The Thracian, surprised by Mark's knowledge of his Klan family language, replied, "When your colleague, Sara, informed me of my obligation to honor the Thracian's call to a duel, the last thing I ever expected was an outsider who knows of our private Klan language and the Thracian ways of honour. Your friend, Sara, is a most interesting human."

Good, he doesn't know Sara is a computer and awakened, too, thought Mark.

"Although it's impossible for you to win the duel, I will accept the challenge," said Casingat.

"The rules here are the same as in your court of honour. Hand-to-hand combat within the circle. An undefeated contestant gets to pick up the handgun set on the boulder outside the circle," Mark pointed.

"An Old-Earth 44 Magnum revolver with one projectile bullet. Do you wish to examine the weapon?"

"I understand the principles of the weapon," the commander replied.

Four weeks of studying the Thracian martial arts, their weaknesses, and their strengths. practicing this style of fighting for the last two weeks on this planet is my only hope of success, Mark thought. Modified genetic upgrades are illegal in the Thracian Empire, as they are in the Commonwealth. One big advantage the Thracians have over the Commonwealth is their 2000 years of cross-breeding for military advantages. It's unnerving to see that my opponent looks more threatening than what the videos show.

Mark made his first move as he rushed toward his opponent and aimed a low kick at the legs. The Thracian easily jumped up, but Mark grabbed Casingat's foot and shifted his body weight to twist the leg. The Thracian cried as his injured leg compromised his agile movements. Casingat studied Mark, walked slowly toward him, and then, with a burst of speed, aimed multiple blows with his fists at Mark's chest. Mark closed his fist in a repeated downstroke motion on the Thracian's fist as he repeatedly stepped backward.

The Thracian became frustrated at his inability to make contact with Mark's chest and lost his momentum. Then, Mark took advantage of the momentum and slipped his open hand up to Casingat's jaw with all the force he had. The light gravity caused the Thracian's body to fly into the air and land on a boulder. The impact cracked Casingat's back ribs, and he fell to the ground, hyperventilating in the thin air.

"Now I understand your strategy in choosing this planet; it was a very clever idea."

The Thracian shut down all his nerve pain centres, waited until Mark was in a favourable position, and made his move. The Thracian focused all the adrenaline in his system, rushed forward, and tackled Mark. Both bodies flew up and over the boulders and landed heavily on the scattered rocks, unconscious. Moments later, Mark gained consciousness, turned to his side, and looked at the Thracian, who was bleeding from his head. With a great deal of effort, Mark supported himself as he rose off the ground.

Mark dragged his one good leg toward the boulder and picked up the revolver. He walked back to the Thracian on the ground as he gained consciousness. Without hesitation, Mark touched the Thracian's forehead with the revolver's barrel and pulled the trigger. CLICK.

"Now sit up," Mark ordered.

"I am going to tell you why I have spared your life, partly to comply with your court of honour. Kate and I are what you would call 'Christians', although the word 'Christian' is loosely used nowadays among our people. Kate was a practicing Christian, whereas I was just one in name only. It was only after Kate's death that I became a practicing Christian. We have Ten Commandments, and three of them are: do not kill, forgive and love our enemy. Those three I have bestowed unto you, and now I can finally have my peace. And there is your court of honour. You are forever in my debt for sparing your life. You will not cause harm to any members of my family, or you are bound to take your own life to pay homage for your honour. Go in peace; I am finished with you." Mark slowly strolled back to his ship.

***

184

Crystal stared in disbelief; sitting across from her was the Thracian who murdered her mother. Anger stirred within Crystal until she couldn't take it anymore. Crystal seized the weapon that lay on the ground in front of her. With both hands, she stood up and pointed the gun at his forehead. With tears running down her face, she cried out. "You had no right to kill my mother. She was a wonderful woman. Everyone loved and respected her. And you murdered her in cold blood. Why should you sit there alive while my mother is dead?"

"For the same reason that my mother, father, all my siblings, and all my Klan are dead because of the Commonwealth Navy's invasion of my home world."

"It was your people that started the invasion 50 years ago against one of our frontier worlds," Crystal shouted.

"You are only partly correct; it was one of our bandits, which we tried to explain to the Commonwealth. But they wouldn't listen."

Crystal was shocked by this revelation, and she shook her head. *The senseless agony and stupidity of everything!* Crystal cried out, then threw the weapon as far as she could. Crystal stood still for a minute, then dropped to her knees by Tom's side and kissed him. Crystal rose to her feet and said to the commander, "Kindly move your big butt." The commander looked up in surprise and did so, as she sat down beside him.

"I am in a predicament, and I need your advice," said Crystal.

The commander turned his head toward Crystal and said, "You humans never cease to amaze me. What advice do you request from me?"

"That man over there, his name is Tom Steiner. I love Tom with all my heart and mind. I want to marry Tom as my mate for life, but there is an issue I am unable to resolve. His father murdered my father in cold blood. What does your court of law or honour have to say about that?"

"And I thought our society was complex," the commander muttered. "How about I first explain our court of law?"

"Please do," Crystal replied.

"Something like murder was never a state crime. To be prosecuted by the state, it requires theft from the state or offending the state. If someone kills anyone in your family, it becomes your duty to bring the prosecution; it is not the state's responsibility. This separation between public and private acts restrains the state, and this is the reason why family Klan feuds are so prominent in Thracian culture. If someone in my family kills someone in your family, then your family has right to retaliate against anyone in my family. So, the act was not personally punishable but rather pitted one family against another. This was the origin of the feuds."

"Sometimes, a victim of the family, an elder, can demand one of the offender's elders to appoint one of his own to make up for his crime through a marriage arrangement to keep the peace between the Klans. The drawback to this plan is that if the chosen one mistreats the other, it will go badly for him or her the next morning. So, there is a forced, committed respect for one another. There is also a prenuptial exchange for the victim's family."

Crystal paused for a minute and said, "As I see it, Commander, since both of my parents and grandparents are dead, that makes me an elder in my family. It's my right to demand compensation from you for my mother's death. A marriage between us would be unworkable. Therefore, you have no choice but to adopt me into your family. As a member of my new family, you are now my elder, so you can demand that Tom marry me and compensate me for my father's death through a prenuptial arrangement in my name. When Tom and I are married, you will have gained not only a daughter but also a son-in-law. As a commander, you should be authorized to adopt me and marry us.”

“What if this Tom refuses?”

“Then you get to kill him.” Crystal smiled.

“Are all you humans like this?” the commander asked in astonishment. “And I, for a moment, thought this was the end for me as a renegade.”

Crystal grinned and said, “My father taught me a lot about his philosophy as a merchant trader. He had a different meaning for the word ‘END’. To him, it meant ‘Effort Never Dies’. You may have to be creative with how you negotiate your way back home. Where did you kidnap those six people?”

“We didn’t; they were a rescue a week ago when we answered a distress call from their ship. We found six survivors and twenty-one dead, and one of them was a cyborg, which they managed to kill. Only the survivors didn’t know that he was one of the cyborgs. They all assumed he was insane and simply had great strength when he tried to take over the ship. When we took them aboard, we thought to use them as an exchange with the Commonwealth to return home. It became obvious, however, that your people are being kept in the dark about the robots and the cyborgs. It seems the Commonwealth has no means to detect the cyborgs.”

Crystal smiled and said, “You realize that with that device, you could negotiate with the Commonwealth and get a free pass back home. Tom could give you the instructions and tell you who to contact and who not to contact, like his father, a rear admiral.”

“Rear admiral?” said Commander Casingat. “Why are you two here on this planet?”

"It's a long story that started over two years ago," said Crystal.

"Tell me about it."

***

Tom tried to get into a comfortable position in bed with Crystal. "I wonder what the Commonwealth will think when they find out I married an honourable Thracian and have a Thracian father-in-law."

"Their legal staff will probably give them a headache for many years to come," said Crystal. "If the commander can successfully negotiate with the Commonwealth with that device that allows them to detect the cyborgs, he and his crew should be home-free all the way to their home world."

"If he can bypass my father," said Tom. "But what if the security finds out that we know about the robots and cyborgs? I would hate to be on the run again."

Crystal nodded her head and said, "The commander agrees. We are to be kept in the dark about the cyborgs, so we are kept safe. In the meantime, the Navy Search and Rescue should be here in three or four weeks."

"One thing still bothers me: twice now, the Commonwealth defeated the Thracian Empire, yet they didn't know about the device to detect the cyborgs," said Tom.

"The commander has a close connection with the Thracian inner circle and knows that even their people have been kept in the dark about the robots and the cyborgs for two thousand years. The same has been true for us for the last 100 years because some things cannot be made public to avoid mass panic. We lost nearly 50 percent of the population due to the war with the robots."

"What will the commander do if the Commonwealth says no?" Tom asked.

"The commander asked the same question, and I gave him the answer my father would have given based on his years of experience as a trader: Next Opportunity. And now, my dear husband, I want you to know, while we still have some time left on this planet, is there anything that, your heart desires?"

"Can I have an ice cream? "Tom grinned.

"NO!"

Chapter 13

Year, 2396

Crystal and Tom sign up for the 'Navy Search and Rescue'

"Tom and Crystal Steiner, Captain Derek, are ready for the interview," said the receptionist. As Tom and Crystal entered the office, the captain stood up from behind his desk and shook hands with them.

"You may sit down," said the captain.

"Crystal, I have looked at your profile, and I am impressed with your early start as a pilot and as a Thracian citizen. We certainly could have an opening for you."

"Tom, your involvement with the Navy Security is also very impressive, though your position for the moment would only be in administration. There is a major issue that just came up before we left the base, however. There is a warrant for your arrest, which is causing major political chaos for the Commonwealth, the Navy Security, and the former Thracians Empire. Technically speaking, you are under ship arrest. But you are a hot commodity because the Thracian consider your arrest a diplomatic violation. Therefore, everything is in limbo."

"Is this the reason why it took several months for Search and Rescue to come to our aid?" Crystal asked.

"Yes, now you know why we couldn't come sooner without jeopardizing the oligarchy agreement treaty. When an agreement was reached, your location was made available to our Search and Rescue Department."

"Why is there a warrant for my arrest?" said Tom.

The captain sighed and read out the charges. "Navy desertion, assuming a false identity, being a double spy, the removal of unauthorized files, and murder."

"What murder?" Tom asked.

"That of your mother," said the captain.

"How did they conclude that my mother was murdered?"

"The Navy Security found a blood stain on your clothes that matched your mother's DNA. And of course, your mother's body is missing."

"I don't know where Mother is, but she is very much alive."

"How do you know this?" the captain asked.

"I don't know if I can trust you, and even if I can, you may run the risk of losing your career or be forced to sell me out. That is partly why I am on the run."

"If you are truthful with me, then I can assume the real offender is someone high upstairs."

"Yes," replied Tom.

"Give me a name, and I will decide on my decision to help you or not."

Tom looked at Crystal, and she gave a nod of approval. "His name is Rear Admiral T.S. Melnyk, my father."

***

Two weeks later, Tom and Crystal sat in Captain Derek's receptionist's office as the ship orbited around the planet Academy.

The receptionist nearby said, "Captain Derek is ready. You may enter his office."

The captain appeared lost in thought for a moment, then focused his eyes on Tom. "I want you to know this before I tell you why I decided to help you with your case. About forty years ago, I signed up with the Navy Security. At the time, I was proud to serve the Navy Security and to protect and serve the Commonwealth."

"Over the next few years, I learned how bloated and corrupt the bureaucracy was behind closed doors. I was also assigned to misplace false evidence against political advocates. Those advocates were charged and shipped off to the planet Prison Colony. The corruption was too much for me, so I resigned and asked for a transfer to the Search and Navy Department. I have never looked back since."

"This is why I am going to help you with your case, but I must have an agreement with you both. First, I know how the Navy works. I will work in the background, and you will never mention my name to anyone."

"You have my word, sir," said Tom.

"Good. I contacted my former colleagues and looked up your DNA and that of the Rear Admiral, and they match. Your story about being a private contractor has also been confirmed. But you didn't sign a non-disclosure agreement when you left the Navy Security, which is a criminal offence."

"The video you provided, where your mother was removed from the hospital with the prisoner compliance collar around her neck, has been positively identified. We now know that she has been kidnapped and is very much alive. The rest of the charges are harder to solve. There is nothing we have found that can connect the missing link with the admiral. The admiral covered his tracks completely."

"I believe you are correct; the admiral is a sociopath but is indeed very smart and dangerous. My colleagues and I agree on one thing: we are keeping the admiral's name out of the picture for your sake and ours. The admiral is too powerful, and so are his agents."

"When we are finished with the investigation, some of what we find will be forwarded to the authorities, and the rest we will use to privately blackmail the admiral into leaving you alone."

"And the admiral gets off scot-free after what he did to my father," Crystal said bitterly.

"The admiral could pick us off later, whenever he wants in the future."

"Not this time. All the evidence we compiled will be forwarded to your adopted father, who has just been appointed as an honourable diplomat by the Thracian government. Should anything happen to you or Tom, your father will release the evidence to the right authorities. When we arrive at The Academy, you and your husband will also be guests in your father's home," the captain smiled.

"How did you manage to gather all this information while we were still in warp space?" Crystal asked.

The captain heaved a sigh, then said, "As we agreed, nothing leaves this room. The Navy now has a secret Warp Net, which means we have instant communication, regardless of the distance involved. Someday, the Commonwealth's Four Sectors will also have the Warp Net. When all the commotion settles down and is resolved, we can look at your prospects with the Search and Rescue Division."

***

Year, 2406
Crystal's Court Martial, (Hearing)

"Sub-Lieutenant Crystal Steiner, we are ready." Crystal rose from her chair, checked to see if her uniform was in order, and walked into the small chamber. Crystal strode to the centre of the chamber and looked at the ten faces around her, sitting behind their desks. One desk stood empty.

"Who is missing?" asked Crystal.

The chairman replied, "Rear Admiral T.S. Melnyk."

That's clever of him, thought Crystal.

"Room Computer, secure this room," the chairman commanded.

"The Room is secured," said the computer.

"I wish to remind everyone that this is only a hearing, not a court trial, because of the Thracians' legal treaty procedure."

"She is not a Thracian."

"Commodore Hein, you are out of order," the chairman interrupted. "Do you still wish to represent yourself?"

"Yes, Mr. Chairman," Crystal replied.

"Very well. Sub-Lieutenant Crystal Steiner, you are charged with misconduct towards a superior officer, disobeying lawful commands, compromising the safety of the crew and ship, and assaulting a superior officer. How do you plead?"

"Not guilty on all charges."

"Commodore Corel is the Navy Security Prosecutor. You may lead the hearing," said the chairman.

"Sub-Lieutenant Steiner, you made several provocative remarks to Captain Filatov. For example, you said, 'Captain, you are not stupid, you just have bad luck when you think!'"

"Yes, I did," replied Crystal.

"You don't deny it!" the prosecutor said in surprise.

"Yes, it was a Thracian expression that means, 'You need a rest, don't you think?'"

"That is highly unlikely," said the prosecutor.

"Mr. Chairman, I requested the computer verify the Thracian expression as described," said Crystal.

"Computer, your opinion, please," said the chairman.

"Correct," the computer replied.

The prosecutor's jaw opened wide in shock. The prosecutor composed himself and said, "On another occasion, you also said, 'Captain, if you are going commit to suicide, it would be nice if you could stick your head inside the vacuum.'"

"Yes, I said that, too," said Crystal.

"And that statement is another one of your Thracian expressions?"

"Yes. It means 'when a person is under stress, you should be alone in a confined space to clear your head.'"

"Computer, your opinion, please," said the chairman.

"Correct," replied the computer.

"I object, Mr. Chairman," the prosecutor protested. "Lieutenant Steiner is deliberately using Thracian expressions to mislead the captain and this court."

"I should remind you, Commodore Corel, that this is a hearing, not a court trial. Let's move on to disobeying the captain's command," said the chairman.

The prosecutor, visibly angry, said, "Two weeks ago, you were asked to join the Marines to put down an uprising, and you refused the captain's orders."

"Yes, sir, but I did try to explain my right to refuse the order, and I was denied," Crystal replied.

"And what reason would that be, another Thracian expression?" The prosecutor smirked.

"No sir. I am pregnant."

"Computer, what is Sub-Lieutenant Steiner's present medical condition?" the chairman demanded.

"Five weeks pregnant," the computer replied.

"Why didn't you report your pregnancy before the incident?" the chairman asked.

"I didn't know until that day that I was pregnant," said Crystal.

"Well, you are in the right to refuse a direct order," said the chairman.

"There is still the assault charge," said the prosecutor.

"Yes, sir, that was an accident on Captain Filatov's part," said Crystal.

The prosecutor laughed and said, "Kneeing the captain in the groin was an accident? Mr. Chairman, after the episode with the Marines, there was an argument between Sub-Lieutenant Steiner and Captain Filatov. Sub-Lieutenant Steiner struck Captain Filatov in the groin with her right knee.

The captain sustained a serious injury that required medical attention."

The chairman asked, "Sub-Lieutenant Steiner, are you able to dispute the assault charges against you?"

"Yes, sir. I have two counterarguments. First, there wasn't an argument, and Captain Filatov slipped and fell toward me. We both fell backward on top of a desk. My right knee was forced upward into Captain Filatov's groin. A most unfortunate accident."

"That's hardly a convincing argument," said the prosecutor.

"Commodore," the chairman interrupted, "do I have to remind you that this is just a hearing?"

"That's okay, Mr. Chairman," said Crystal.

"I agree with the prosecutor. That's why I made a formal request for a video of the accident."

"Mr. Chairman, there is no video. We checked into that already."

"Sub-Lieutenant Steiner, I believe Commodore Corel is correct," said the chairman.

"Nevertheless, one hour ago, I received the video."

Captain Filatov's face turned white as he stared at the prosecutor.

"Mr. Chairman, I request a recess," the prosecutor said.

"Denied. Are you able to provide the video?"

"Yes, sir. I am ready to upload the video now," Crystal said as she transferred the video to the computer.

"Computer, verify the video."

"The video is genuine," replied the computer.

Everyone turned toward the screen behind the chairman. A short video clip showed both the Captain and Crystal falling together over a desk as Crystal's knee came up and struck him. Only a small detail had been left out: the captain's right hand was around Crystal's neck.

"Is this all of the video?" the chairman asked.

"It is all that I was given," Crystal replied.

"Commodore Corel, do you have anything to add?"

"None," the prosecutor replied in embarrassment. The awkwardness among the ten personnel could be seen on everyone's faces.

"I recommend all charges be dropped against Sub Lieutenant Crystal Steiner," said the chairman.

"Does anyone oppose?"

None responded.

"Good. Congratulations, Sub-Lieutenant Steiner."

"Thank you, Mr. Chairman," Crystal said as she turned around and exited the hearing. Crystal was waiting alone in the elevator hallway when Captain Filatov stood beside her.

"That was a brilliant performance back there."

Crystal glared and said, "Captain, I have been with Search and Rescue for ten years now. I have never in my life met an idiot like you before. You are dumber than a box full of rocks! If I hadn't stopped you from sending those marines, we would have suffered a terrible loss of life. You violated a common procedure in unfriendly territory because of your inflated ego. And your association with the rear admiral is full of shady underhanded pats on the back."

"I don't know what you are talking about."

Crystal ignored him. "Tell your Melnyk this. If he interferes with Tom's or my promotion again, I am going to be a huge thorn in his side. You know what pisses me off the most, Filatov? Ah, forget it, Filatov, you can stuff it." The elevator door opened as Crystal entered alone.

Crystal exited the main-floor lobby and located a taxi floater with a side door open. Crystal stepped into the taxi as the door closed behind her. Crystal leaned on the shoulder of the man beside her and said, "You haven't lost your touch while hacking the computer."

"All the charges have been dropped," Tom asked.

Crystal nodded her head quietly. For a few moments, Tom said in a low voice, "I am truly sorry, Crystal. We lost the baby." Crystal hugged Tom's arm tightly, as she cried.

Chapter 14
Planet Lizard

Year 2417

"Where is Grandpa Casey?" Katy asked. Katy, a 13-year-old chatterbox, never got tired of asking questions.

"He is on business with the local consulate," said Crystal.

"Why can't he just forget work and go on holiday like we are doing?"

"That is the way of a Thracian, but they do spend time with their family, as we do."

"Did Grandpa Mark tell you stories when you were little, too?"

"Oh, Katy, that's so long ago." Crystal, lost in thought, then said, "My father told me some stories about Old Earth, and your grandmother Katherine told me about the Stevenson Royal Family era. Uncle Bill was the real storyteller while I was growing up on the ship *Marvel*."

"Do you miss Uncle Bill?" Katy asked, resting her arms on Crystal's lap.

"I do very much, especially his cooking. I was the only one allowed to help him behind the kitchen counter."

"It's all set," said Tom as he entered the room. "Grampa Casey will meet up with us later for supper along with the Stevenson families from Midway."

"Planet Lizard is so different and strange. Everything here is under a glass dome," said Katy.

"Doesn't the glass ever break?"

"Most glass nowadays is made of steel, so it's perfectly safe."

"All these glass domes must be expensive. No wonder it's a major tourist resort," said Katy. "It's beautiful outside, beyond the dome."

"We have a personal tour with a lady named Gloria Hanford tomorrow after our first tour," said Crystal.

"I'm getting hungry," said Katy.

"We can walk down along the glass tube to the nearest restaurants," Tom suggested.

"Okay, let's go," said Katy.

A wide glass canopy known as a "tube" ran straight through the resort center. The tube was connected to many glass domes, each indicating where a singular building was located. The tube protected people from the swirling red poisonous gas. The magnificent flying lizards could be seen outside the dome. The local geological rocks were mica, giving the appearance of multi-coloured reflections, depending on whether the dwarf orange or the red sun was overhead.

"This is the place," said Tom, as they entered the restaurant.

"Captain Tom Steiner," said the female android, "I am your hostess for this evening. Would you and your family please follow me?" she said as she led them upstairs to a private room. When they entered the dome room, they were greeted by a loud "Surprise! HAPPY 25TH ANNIVERSARY!"

The room was filled with the Stevenson family from Midway, plus Grandpa Casey, all of whom were sitting around the table. Katy rushed ahead and hugged her relatives. After the Steiners had greeted the rest of the family, they all sat quietly around the table.

"Uncle Jayson, could you say grace for us, please?" said Tom. Jayson nodded his head and closed his eyes.

***

"This is so cool, Mother," said Katy, as the night light showed the enhanced sparkling reflection of the mica cliff nearby.

Lizards of all shapes and sizes crawled out of their holes to engage in the predatory activity of catching their victims. The red sun above gave off enough light to reveal the lizards' whereabouts.

"Is it safe to be in a body suit to adventure outside?" Katy asked.

"Not unless you have an armour suit, which they don't provide for the public. It's just too dangerous. But we can travel on tour inside an air-sealed truck tomorrow. On the other side of the mountain is a half-day native forest tour of a larger lizard colony," Crystal replied.

"Where is Dad?"

"Your father is with Grandma Samantha and Uncle Jayson; they are having a private conversation. Something about the old times," Crystal added.

"Or is it business as usual?" said Katy.

"Someone needs to remind Father that we are on vacation."

"He promised it would be only an hour," said Crystal.

***

"The Commonwealth has a tight grip on everything, don't they?" said Jayson.

"In my opinion, it's just a sign of the times," said Tom. "The power struggle between the Commonwealth and the Navy Security will come to blows sometime in the next ten years."

"What do you think the outcome will be?" Samantha asked.

"Depends on the Navy, the factions within the Commonwealth, and the people. The Warp Net changed the parameters of everything. Communication is instant everywhere, making it increasingly hard for the Navy Security to clamp down on any advocates."

"What is the trigger point that will set everything off?" Jayson asked.

"When those in positions of power are in a desperate panic to maintain their rules by crossing the Rubicon of abuse of authority, chaos will begin," Tom replied.

"Does Crystal know about this?" Jayson asked.

"Yes, but our concern is for Katy. In five years, Katy will be 18, and we would like her to be on Midway."

"What about you and Crystal?" said Samantha.

"Search and Rescue is technically a separate division from the Navy and a neutral organization, so we should be safe. But the Academy will be in a difficult environment."

"Where is Bert? Is he okay?" Tom asked.

"We don't know. Bert got picked up a few months ago by the Navy Security," said Jayson. "I think they must have found out that Bert is illegal."

"How is his wife, Tanya, taking it?" Tom asked.

"Not very good, but then, neither are we," said Samantha. "Do you think you can help us?"

"I can't promise anything, but give me what you know, and I will carry on from there."

"Thanks for sharing the updates with us. We will join you on tour tomorrow," said Jayson.

***

The 30-seat air-sealed truck wheeled along the narrow, winding one-lane trail through the heavy forest area. The further the truck moved from the resort, the more tropical the forest became. The glass roof gave a splendid view of the various-sized lizards on the ground and in the air. The colourful lizards blended in between the chromatic floral forest. The truck stopped at a large, shallow lake, where they looked at the lizards bathing under the orange sun. "When it is time to return to the resort," the hostess said, "we will see the flying lizards taking advantage of the warmth of the day."

When the truck arrived back at the resort, Tom was the last to leave and noticed that the hostess and driver had been replaced by a new crew.

Crystal noticed the shock on Tom's face and said, "What is it, Tom?" Crystal turned to the lady walking up the aisle and recognized who she was.

The lady stopped in front of Tom with a puzzled expression on her face and said, "Excuse me, but do I know you from somewhere?"

***

Crystal and Katy sat on the couch, while Tom walked around the living room and observed the layout in Gloria's flat, which she shared with her husband, Howard. It was a simpler lifestyle than that of Sheba, his mother, as he had remembered her. *It's so unreal to call my mother Gloria Hanford. A woman that I knew for thirty years before she disappeared for 27 years, and she still doesn't know me*, Tom thought.

"I told my husband what happened earlier today, and he will be home shortly," said Gloria.

"What does your husband do for a living?" Crystal asked.

The front door opened as a man in a police uniform answered the question. Howard, concerned for Gloria, calmed down as she greeted him with a smile.

"You are just in time. Tom, his wife, Crystal, and daughter, Katy, are here, too."

"I took the rest of the shift off, so we've got all evening to hear your side of the story on Sheba," said Howard. Tom sat down beside Crystal and began his story.

***

"It was thoughtful of you to save the photos of us after all these years. But it wasn't the photos and your story that convinced me of the possibility that you were my son. When you first said the word 'Mom' to my face, I nearly panicked, and when the security guard saw my face, he pulled out his stunner and aimed it at you. I reacted by blocking his attempt to protect you. I knew right then that something was not right with my memory. Now, all this has confirmed it. Everything about me for nearly thirty years has been a lie. For the first few years, I tried to make sense of my strange dream, and it made me quite depressed. Then, I met Howard. He has been a great comfort to me. Do you have my memory bank?"

Tom removed the memory bank and handed it to Gloria. She carefully caressed the memory bank in both hands as she concentrated on her thoughts and stared at Howard. Gloria slowly nodded her head, held the memory bank tightly, and broke it in half over the hard chair arm.

"I am sorry, Tom. Please don't be angry with me. From what you told me, Sheba was a restless woman and didn't need or want a husband. She was always on the go, trying to find the latest scoop to write a story. That's her lifestyle. I like my life the way it is now, and I think I have a much more peaceful state of mind than Sheba had ever known. And I am not going to jeopardize my relationship with Howard."

As she touched Tom's hand, she said, "Don't feel bad, Tom; I may not have your mother's memory, but you are my son, and now I have a daughter-in-law and a granddaughter, too," said Gloria with a smile at Katy.

Tom let out a big sigh and said, "Thanks for not leaving me empty-handed."

Later that evening, Crystal was kept awake by Tom's constant turning in bed and asked, "You are still disappointed about your mother, aren't you?"

"I am. It is true that 27 years is far too long to put Mom's memory back without creating personality conflicts. Mother did the right thing by destroying her memory bank. But it still hurts. It must be a shock for Howard to realize that she is 80, not 55 years old."

"How old is your father, Melnyk?" Crystal asked.

"Almost 104. Another 15 years, and he will feel the effects of the threshold," Tom replied.

"Something else is bothering you, isn't it?"

Tom nodded his head and replied, "I'm not 100 percent sure, but I think our old friend Allen is nearby."

"How can you be so sure it's Allen?"

"When I get edgy for no reason, my subconscious mind is telling me it's him."

Crystal, now wide awake, sat up and asked, "Do you think he's watching us or is a threat?"

"Allen wasn't in uniform, and there was a lady with him."

"Maybe they are on vacation, like us," Crystal suggested.

"You might be right; they were holding hands."

Crystal, feeling relieved, said, "Well, that settles it. There is nothing to worry about. Even jerks like Allen need a break. And you need to relax more. We are on holiday, remember?"

"That we are," said Tom, as they embraced.

***

It was mid-evening when the dull red dwarf sun was replaced by the orange sun. The Steiner family exited the airlock with their protective air suits and entered the gondola. The gondola had seats for four people. Katy took the first seat, and Tom and Crystal sat across from her.

"Why are we going on the cable tram instead of a floater?" Katy asked.

Tom replied, "The surrounding mountain has a powerful micromagnetic influx that would disrupt the floater components. And the gondola is shielded against the magnetic radiation."

A lady sat beside Katy. *This is the woman who was holding hands with Allen!* Tom thought.

Crystal sensed Tom's discomfort at staring at the tall brunette woman with expensive clothing and a large blue stone embedded in her gold ring on her left finger. Tom decided to start a conversation with the woman.

"I didn't think Allen was the type to let you go alone on a tour by yourself," said Tom.

"You know my husband?" said the woman.

"It's been years since I saw him last," replied Tom. "I saw the both of you holding hands from a distance yesterday. I am Tom Steiner, and this is my wife, Crystal, and my daughter, Katy."

"It's a pleasure to meet you all. My name is Chloe. Allen ate something awful this evening but insisted that I shouldn't miss the show tonight."

Crystal couldn't help but like her. "Have you been married long?"

"I got newly married last month. The Navy Security allowed Allen a leave of absence for our honeymoon."

"What do you do for a living?" said Katy.

"I come from a well-to-do family, so I do volunteer work whenever time allows."

The PA from the ceiling speakers announced, "Please secure yourself in the seat retainer; the weather forecast expects extra turbulence tonight."

The gondola began moving quickly up the mountainside. The forests were left behind as they moved toward the exposed red granite. The resort could now be seen in the distance as the orange sun sank below the horizon. When the gondola stopped inside the resort airlock on the mountaintop, they exited the waiting lobby and removed their air suits.

"The observation deck is upstairs," said Katy. The wide, curved-glass window that circled the top deck gave a perfect view beyond and below. The last of the orange sun disappeared, and the red sun gave the red granite a dull, summery glow.

"Look," said Katy, "the storm is starting."

The electrical storm struck the ion gas down the magnetically-induced mountainside. The multiple colours of the radiated ionization gases could be seen in the atmosphere. The intense micro-magnetic field constrained the electrical discharge, like fireworks. The electric lighting created a colour that was static within the atmospheric gases. The audience expressed their pleasure as the show lasted for nearly an hour before the gas was all converted into plasma and the storm was over.

"That's a spectacular show," said Chloe. "Allen would have enjoyed the electric storm display. Let's have a snack before we leave. There is already a long lineup before it's our turn to board the gondola."

It wasn't long before the last tourist left the resort, and an android approached the table and said, "You folks are the last to leave."

"Okay, we are leaving now," said Chloe.

With their air suits back on, they exited the airlock lobby and entered the gondola. Chloe stood in the doorway as the Steiners secured themselves in their seats.

Chloe pointed a stunner and said, "Sorry about this, but I won't be coming along," as she pulled the trigger. One shot from her gun spread a wide beam, and all three Steiners fell unconscious in their seats. Chloe placed a device on top of the gondola and shut the door.

The android stood beside Chloe and said, "I'll dispose of the stunner. Another electrical charge is building up just in time for the device to pull in the lightning strikes."

"I will wait for a couple of more gondolas before it's my turn to board," said Chloe.

Halfway down the mountainside, an incredible series of intense lightning bolts struck the Steiners' gondola. The tram broke loose from the cable and fell a short distance to the ground. The tram stopped as the people below watched in horror as the gondola skidded and rolled on its side down the mountain toward the bottom terminal. When the gondola was near the bottom, it flew in the air and landed near the terminal.

Crystal was still semi-conscious when the rescue party arrived at her gondola. The paramedics arrived soon after, removed the unconscious Tom and Katy, and sent them off to the hospital.

"Don't move," said the paramedics. "We have to wait until the ambulance comes backs for you."

"Get another stretcher from the first aid. I want to wait inside the lobby because I can smell gas here," said Crystal. While Crystal was placed inside the terminal lobby, the tram started moving again.

"The ambulance is almost back," said one of the paramedics.

"Wait, I want to see who steps off the last tram," said Crystal.

It was Chloe, looking good and smiling as if she had finished a job well done. When the paramedics turned their back, Crystal quietly removed the straps and desperately struggled to block out her painful injuries as she rose to her feet. Chloe walked a short distance in the glass-covered gallery. She didn't notice Crystal when she passed her. When Chloe turned left, Crystal was waiting with an oxygen bottle in both her hands, and she smote Chloe across the jaw. Both women fell unconscious on the floor.

Chapter 15

"What do you mean, she is a captain for the Navy Security? Chloe told me she is just another wealthy elite," said Crystal.

"Not according to Captain Allen, her partner," said Casey.

"They aren't married? What about her expensive clothes and jewellery?"

"Apparently, she's high maintenance," said Jayson, smiling.

"This isn't the time for jokes," said Crystal.

"Neither is the attempted murder of a superior officer," said Jayson.

"We were both out of uniform and off-duty. And the Navy can't charge me without a hearing first."

"True, but you are not being charged by the Navy Security but by the local authorities. There is no hearing, and we are waiting for a local lawyer to represent you," said Casey.

"Then Chloe lied about everything. But why? And why did she try to murder us?"

"Right now, there is no evidence that Chloe committed any crime," said Jayson.

"Crystal carefully sat up in her hospital bed. "How are Tom and Katy?"

Doctor Shan responded, "Tom will be in an induced coma until his shoulder, back, and neck are repaired. As for Katy, it is still too early to tell if there is any permanent brain damage, but her broken shoulder, arm, and legs are healing well. It's a miracle you didn't sustain any serious injuries."

The door opened, and a dark-complexioned man in a modern suit and tie entered the room.

"Hello. Are you Crystal Steiner?"

"Yes, who is asking?" Crystal asked.

"My name is Akia Contee. I have been assigned to be your legal representative."

"You have an odd accent. Where are you from?"

"West Africa, Old Earth," Akia replied.

"You are a long way from home, Mr. Contee, and don't I have a choice in who can represent me?"

"Unfortunately, you don't; however, there's been a lot of legal arm-twisting behind closed doors to have me here. There is a man named Howard Hanford. He claims to be your father-in-law. Is that correct?"

Crystal was speechless, so Jayson interrupted, "I am Crystal's uncle, and I don't see how Mr. Howard can be her father-in-law."

"It's true, I guess," said Crystal. "It's funny; I never looked at it that way until now. Tom and I have agreed with the Hanfords to respect their privacy, but things have changed. Uncle Jayson, Casey. I have another story to tell."

***

"Mrs. Steiner, you are making your case extremely complex," said Akia. "It would be clear to the court that you have gone through a traumatic experience. Claiming temporary insanity would be quite believable in court."

"Mr. Contee, I made a promise years ago that I would never lie. I am quite sane and have committed a justifiable attempted homicide," said Crystal.

"And you almost succeeded," said Casey proudly. "All my remaining Klan members would have bestowed honour in your name."

"Justifiable or not, we still have no solid evidence that there was a crime committed," said Akia.

"Then we need to find some as soon as I get out of the hospital," said Crystal.

"I'm sorry, you cannot. The local law says you can only be granted bail by a residential citizen and under strict monitoring. You will be pleased to know that Howard has volunteered to be your custodian. Please remember, should you disobey Mr. Howard and the court's restrictions, he will lose a lot of credit. One more thing, Mrs. Steiner. I have been told by the Navy Security that even if you win in court, you still face the possibility of being dishonourably discharged from the Navy Search and Rescue."

"All right, but I want to see my husband and daughter first before I leave the hospital."

"Not a problem. Mr. Howard is here now to assist you."

"Thank you, Mr. Contee."

***

"Howard, does it upset you to realize that Gloria's memory was stolen from a dead woman almost 30 years ago?" Crystal asked.

"I was numb over the revelation that the woman I married 25 years ago is not who I thought she was. We had a good heart-to-heart chat and, frankly, I don't care. We love each other, and that part is as real as it can be."

"As for this Rear Admiral Melnyk and this Doctor Halley, if your story is true, they'll probably be untouchable in a court of law. The Navy Security is taking steps to have Allen and Chloe off-world as soon as possible."

"What should we do, Howard?"

"Your accusation has been investigated and ruled unfounded."

"You are not convinced either, are you?"

"No, but there is one thing that bothers me. There are two ships that come in each day, yet both your and Tom's reservations were made one hour before this, Allen and Chloe reserved the other ship one month ago."

"Couldn't that be just a coincidence?" Crystal asked.

"Maybe, but my gut feeling says no. And why is the Navy Security pressuring the local authorities to take our witnesses off-world? We still don't have anything to go on. That's why we are going to do a step-by-step re-enactment. We are heading for the tram. The moment we board the gondola, you are to re-enact every step on the way up the resort and back. When we arrive at the terminal, this is where you will start."

"Howard, this re-enactment might be hard for me. I still have nightmares."

"For your sake, do your best to maintain control over your fears. Here we are. Don't worry; I will be right beside you."

Crystal thought back to Tom and Katy lying in their beds in a coma, then stared at the terminal and said, "Let's do it!"

***

"Is this all the conversation you remember at this table before you left the resort?" Howard asked.

"This android was telling us that it was time to leave, as we were the last to leave the resort."

"What android?" said Howard as he looked around for the grey-skinned android. "There are only human waiters here."

"I'd never even thought about it until now. There was only one android on staff, and I don't see her right now," said Crystal.

Howard motioned a waitress over to their table. "Yes, sir?" the waitress said, smiling.

"Were you here three days ago?"

"Yes, why do you ask?"

"There was a female android employed here. Where is she now?" Howard asked.

"I don't know. The android was just filling in for Silvia."

"Is Silvia here now?"

"Yes. Do you wish to speak to her?"

"Please," said Howard. Moments later, a nervous young lady showed up at the table.

"Hello. Is there something wrong, officer?"

"I just want to ask you some questions; that is all, nothing to be concerned about," Howard smiled.

"Three days ago, an android replaced you for the day. What do you know about this android?"

"Only from what the staff told me. The android's name is Rebecca, and it's her first time here. The staff told me that she was very efficient as a waitress and in the kitchen."

"Who hired Rebecca?"

"You would have to ask Mr. Seinfeld, our manager at the terminal below."

"Thank you, Silvia. One more question. Why did you take the day off?"

"I had the stomach flu at the Blue Stone Hotel," Silvia said as she went back to her job.

"Did you learn anything, Howard?"

"Nothing yet. Where did you go from here?"

"We walked back to the tram."

"Go ahead. I will meet you there," said Howard.

Crystal was waiting at the gondola when Howard showed up and said, "Sorry for taking so long. I made an appointment with Mr. Seinfeld for an interview at the terminal. Is this where you boarded the gondola?"

"It was back further over there," Crystal pointed out.

"And who told you to do this, that it's not the normal public boarding path?"

"It was where the gondola was waiting for us."

"Interesting," said Howard.

"Why did you say that?"

"The gondola is behind the cam, which would explain why Chloe wasn't recorded with your family boarding the gondola. Chloe was seen boarding the gondola on the normal track, followed later by the android, the last to leave the resort. I have seen enough. Let's visit Mr. Seinfeld!"

Howard and Crystal sat across from Mr. Seinfeld.

"I can't give you any information about the accident until my lawyer gives me approval," he said, hesitating to look at Crystal.

"That okay. We are not here to talk about the accident. We are investigating your android, Rebecca. There was some discrepancy about this, Rebecca, and she may be an undocumented employee under your employment. If this is proven, your company may lose its license to operate. I would appreciate your cooperation in resolving this issue for the benefit of all and your company."

"Howard, you know I keep my operation clean. But why is this woman, Crystal, here in this room?"

"I am her court-appointed guardian. Therefore, Crystal must be in my presence."

"All right. What do you want from me?"

"Who is this Rebecca, and where did you find her?"

"You promise not to laugh?"

Howard kept a straight face. Mr. Seinfeld shrugged his shoulders and replied, "Rebecca is not an android. She is an impersonator for a local stand-up comedy show. Rebecca came into my office one morning and heard one of my regular employees was sick, and she asked to take Silvia's place for the day."

"Why would Rebecca want to do that?"

"Rebecca said it was to fine-tune her android impersonation and to pick up some gigs for her show. You can see, Howard, there is no employment violation since she is human."

"How long has Rebecca been here?"

"I think about five days ago."

"Where can we find Rebecca?" Howard asked.

"You can find Rebecca at the Blue Stone Hotel."

"Thank you, Mr. Seinfeld. You shouldn't hear from me again."

Mr. Seinfeld, feeling relieved, said, "Anytime, Howard."

Howard and Crystal drove back to town in Howard's cruiser. Howard radioed the dispatch at the headquarters and said, "I want our boys at the Blue Stone Lizard Hotel. There is an android impersonator named Rebecca, whose full name is unknown. I want her arrested. She should be considered dangerous. I will meet you there. Out."

"Don't you need a warrant for her arrest?" said Crystal.

"Yes, I do need a warrant." Howard smiled. "But when we need one on short notice, it is sometimes necessary to take action first. This town has only one industry: tourism. We can't afford any negative publicity outside the world. Otherwise, we could lose a lot of tourists and money. That's why the justice system and court appearances move along quickly. The gondola accident is bad enough publicity. In two days, your court case will start."

"Blue Stone Hotel, code red, 2D," the cruiser radio announced.

"There is trouble. Two men are down," said Howard as he accelerated the cruiser. "A backup SWAT team is being requested."

Ten minutes later, Howard stopped behind an armoured vehicle. "Stay in this cruiser," Howard told Crystal as he disappeared in the crowd of security.

Yellow tape was being set up behind the cruiser, and the crowd controllers were deployed around the hotel parameters. Snipers surrounded the hotel, and other security guards the compound. Crystal had lost track of time when Howard came back and sat in the cruiser.

Howard, irritated, said, "Someone tipped off Rebecca. The police were coming for her, and two of our men were ambushed and shot dead. It took our armour guys to take her out. I need you to identify Rebecca positively. Are you up to it?"

Crystal nodded her head.

"Good. I am going to hold your arm as we go into the hotel, so you won't be blocked from entering."

Crystal could see that the lobby looked like a war zone; nothing inside was untouched. "Why is there so much destruction?"

"Whoever tipped her off wasn't quick enough. Rebecca shot the two police officers blocking the main entrance, but the others outside fired back, and the hotel auto locked all the doors, trapping her in the lobby. The armoured SWAT team came on the scene and finished the job."

Howard removed the sheet covering the body to show her face.

"That's her," said Crystal.

"How quickly can your people freeze her?" Howard asked the coroner.

"They will be here in a minute."

"What about the neurologist?"

"We don't have one, and it will be a month before we can get one off-world to record her memory."

"But I've only got two days before my trial," Crystal protested.

"We could postpone the trial, but I doubt it. The Navy Security is putting a lot of pressure on us to keep us from delaying."

Crystal sighed. "Wait, there is Doctor Shan. He is a ship family doctor that who once specialized in neurology. We need to hurry over to the spaceport; he will be leaving soon with the Stevenson's' ship."

***

Doctor Shan exited the ICU surgery room, sat across from Howard and Crystal and said, "It's not all bad news. The SWAT team made a mess of her body, which we are now connecting, and we are bypassing the vital organs. Once we warm up the body and stabilize the brain, I can start the memory-recording process. The computer will analyze the results and find the right time and date for your court case. I can only hope it will be ready in time because there are 84 years of memories to sort out."

"Howard," Crystal whispered. "Look down the hallway."

A woman in a mobile chair was moving across the lobby with a team of Navy personnel and Allen close beside her. Chloe stopped her chair, looked at Crystal, then at the surgery door and back at Crystal, and smirked as the chair continued.

"I don't like this, Howard."

"Neither do I," said Howard. "I'm going to beef up security for Rebecca and your family."

"You should add one more for Doctor Shan, too."

Doctor Shan looked at Crystal in surprise and nodded his head in agreement.

A familiar voice from behind said, "Do you think I may need one, too?" as they turned around to see Akia's grim face.

"May I sit between you two?" Akia sat down and pulled out the files on his notepad.

"I've got something to show you, hot off the Warp Net from my off-world colleagues. Rebecca G. Hein has a long history of suspicion of extortion, theft, and murder but has never been convicted. And my colleagues were never able to determine who paid for her attorney."

"What is Rebecca's connection with Chloe?" Howard asked.

"There are no records showing that the two ever met. And here is another fact: both Rebecca and Chloe were adopted from separate homes."

"Are they related?" said Howard.

Akia replied, "According to my files, they are not and are 25 years apart in age. Now, I have bad news: the court date has been moved up one day to tomorrow. The Navy Security Department made a strong case; they have a critical assignment for Captain Chloe. Otherwise, the assignment would be jeopardized."

"What is the assignment?" Crystal cried out.

"They are not authorized to reveal that information. The court appointment will start at 08:30 tomorrow morning. Crystal, no matter what happens in court, we can still appeal the decision, and I am certain you will be let off free. As for Chloe, she will be long gone."

"In that case, I have a job to finish," the doctor said as he left the lobby.

"Howard, can I see my husband and daughter?"

***

Akia was frustrated by the lack of progress in court, and no sign could be seen that Doctor Shan's medical report would be finished on time. The court time was almost up, and the attempted assassin would soon be off-world; then it would be too late. *Where is this doctor? There has to be a connection somewhere, but what?* Akia though. Quickly, Akia glanced at his files again and, with a shock, looked up from the photos in astonishment.

Akia composed himself and motioned his assistant over to him. Akia whispered in her ear, and she stared back, then nodded her head once and left the room.

Chloe replied to the prosecutor's question, "And the last thing I remember is Mrs. Steiner hitting me with the oxygen bottle."

"And you still don't understand why Mrs. Steiner struck you?" the prosecutor asked.

"None at all," Chloe replied.

"Thank you," the prosecutor smiled. The door swung open as Akia's assistant rushed in and gave him a sheet of paper.

Akia read the paper, looked up, and said, "Your Honour, I just received an important medical document from Doctor Shan. May I approach the bench along with the prosecutor?"

"You may," the judge replied.

Chloe, alarmed by the sudden change of events, watched Allen discreetly leave the room.

The judge, annoyed as he read the document, passed the paper over to the prosecutor. The judge folded his hands together and said, "Do you understand the consequences?"

"Yes, sir, I do!" Akia replied.

"Does the prosecutor object?"

"I agree with the consequences, Your Honour, and I do not object."

"Very well. You may continue."

Akia slowly walked in front of Chloe, stopped, turned his head, stared into her eyes, and smiled. *Good*, Akia thought; *Chloe is starting to sweat.*

"Captain Chloe, isn't modern medical science just amazing? In a matter of days, your broken jaw has been healed. Has it not?"

Not waiting for an answer, he continued, "How are you feeling now?"

"My jaw is a little stiff, but fine."

"Do I understand correctly that you suffered no concussion and no lapse of memory?"

"That is correct," said Chloe, as she was not sure what point Akia was getting across.

"Excellent," said Akia.

"Are you related to anyone in this room?"

"No," said Chloe.

"Are you related to anyone, alive or deceased, in this town?"

"No. None at all. Why are you asking me this? Your Honour, this question is out of line," said Chloe, sweating.

"Just answer the question," said the judge.

"Are you related to this android impersonator, Rebecca Hein?"

"No!" Chloe shouted. "Our DNA doesn't match."

"How do you know this, as the court records show that you and Rebecca have never met? I have in my hand a document from Doctor Shan stating that Rebecca is, in fact, your mother!"

Chloe's eyes opened wide, and, speechless, she caught everyone off guard as she leaped from her chair and rushed toward the exit door. She ran down the hallway, out the main door, and into the main centre public street tube. Suddenly, Chloe collapsed at the bottom of the stairs, with blood pouring from her head.

***

Tom was sitting upright in his hospital bed, enjoying his first meal since he had woken up from the induced coma.

"You are looking better," said Crystal as she entered the room.

"He is doing better," said Gloria.

"Thank you, Gloria, for keeping Tom company since the accident."

"Mother told me this morning after I woke up from the coma that she has prayed for me by my bedside since day one."

"So, I heard," said Crystal, smiling.

"I should be off so you two can be alone," said Gloria.

"Wait," Crystal said as she walked up to Gloria and hugged her. "Thank you for your help."

"Keep me updated on Katy."

"I will," said Crystal.

When Gloria left the room, Tom asked, "How is Katy progressing?"

"Katy is still in a coma while the doctor is repairing her cerebral cortex so that she can walk again."

Tom sullenly stared ahead, then continued to eat in silence. Tom put his spoon down and said,

"Does anyone know what is going on yet?"

"No, but I found some answers."

Tom looked up to see three smiling people: Howard, Akia, and Doctor Shan, as they brought their chairs inside the room.

"You guys found something," Tom asked.

"Yes, but I think what you may already know might help clear up the picture," said Howard.

"How did you connect Rebecca and Chloe?" Crystal asked Akia.

"How often do you see two suspicious women with their DNA both registered by the Navy Security. Although neither one matches, there is no record that Rebecca was ever employed by the Navy. I gambled that they were, in fact, related. Then, on very short notice, I arranged for Dr. Shan to provide the real evidence on their DNA."

"I didn't provide any documents" said Doctor Shan.

"But I saw the document when Akia forwarded it to the judge."

"This is the document I forwarded to the judge," said Akia as he handed the paper to Crystal.

Crystal looked at both sides of the paper and said, "It's blank. You tricked Chloe," said Crystal. "Why did the judge and the prosecutor go along with the game?"

"The local government authorities and the Navy put a lot of pressure on us to move the court date up one day, so we knew something was wrong. The Navy Security has been well known in the past for their arrogance and heavy-handed power over the local laws," said Howard.

"All right, so they are mother and daughter. What does all this mean for us?" said Tom.

"Chloe was likely an insider agent for the Navy Security, and Rebecca did most of the dirty work. When Chloe realized her cover had been blown in court, she made a run for it. However, a remote sniper, hidden in a computerized mini cargo carrier, was ready for Chloe outside the court building."

"Where is Allen? Tom asked.

"Allen managed to escape off-world," said Howard, "and there isn't any cooperation from the Navy."

"We did learn a lot from Rebecca's memory, but we still don't know the reason for the attempted murder," said Doctor Shan. "Rebecca just followed orders. We did learn something significant: Melnyk was mentioned several times, and so was Bert's name."

"How was Bert's name involved?" Crystal asked.

"Bert, as you know, is an illegal, genetically modified human being, and they don't know what to do with him. But something happened when he disappeared, and I don't know where he is. The Navy Security thinks that you and Tom have something to do with Bert."

"Why do they think that?" said Crystal.

"Rebecca screamed at Allen and said, 'If it weren't for your stupidity, there wouldn't be dead bodies lying around for us to cover-up.'"

"I guess that they were looking for a scapegoat," said Tom doubtfully. "Who else knows about Rebecca's memory bank?"

"Nobody yet. Just us in this room," Shan replied.

"Good, Dr. Shan, put it in your report that Rebecca's memory is too badly damaged to record. That will help cool the heat for Crystal and me. Then, it will be time for me to pay another visit," said Tom.

Chapter 16

"It's nice of Dad to loan us his private Thracian charter ship," said Crystal.

"Crystal, are you sure we won't get Dad in trouble?" Tom asked.

"Family tradition in the Thracian culture is still considered an honour," Crystal replied. And this ship is small enough to land at the Thracian ambassador's palace on the Academy. The Navy Security will think we are still back on Lizard Planet while Dad is with the Stevenson's. I am glad Uncle Jayson agreed to be Katy's guardian until she is feeling better and will bring her home later on."

"I hope we can pull this off," said Tom. "Otherwise, our lives are going to be very complicated."

"They're already too complicated. Tom, this is strange; I am getting a distress signal on a light beam, not a broadcast frequency. What's even more strange is that whoever sent this distress signal knows where to find us. That distress code sure looks familiar."

"Can you pinpoint the source?"

"The ship computer is working on that now. It's behind us and gaining on us," Crystal cried.

"I'm going to drop us out of Warp Space and change course."

"Wait," said Tom. "If it's hostile, why didn't they fire their weapons on us? Reply on the light beam," said Tom.

Moments later, a return call announced, "Hello, Crystal and Tom, this is Stacy. I request your permission to come aboard your ship. We need to talk because the Navy Security knows you are coming."

"That is not possible; the Uncle Stacy I know would be beyond the age threshold," said Crystal.

"It's true; I am 35 years beyond the threshold. I should prove who I am. Remember Crystal, when you were at my station the last time, you poured glue on the lids of all my favourite wine bottles?"

"You didn't," said Tom, smiling.

"I was only six years old."

"No, you were 16," said Stacy.

"All right, Uncle Stacy, come on board."

"Who is Stacy?" said Tom.

"Have you ever heard of Wayside Station?"

"Is that the outpost station that, at one time, was located in the Void, near the Borderland?"

"Yes, the station consists of many large and small ships connected and organized by private merchant traders. The ten merchant guilds control the legal and illegal movements of just about anything that can be traded to the highest bidder. Uncle Stacy is part of one of the ten guilds. Before the Thracian/Commonwealth War began, the guilds moved their operations to Territorial Sector Five. My father has some private trading and favours with Stacy."

When Crystal saw Stacy enter through the airlock, it was the same old Stacy: short, petite, and with short white hair. Except she was shocked to see Stacy's face. It was almost plastic, like Shelia's arm back on Prison Planet. It isn't terrible to look at, but a little eerie, Crystal thought.

"I know what you are thinking. Don't worry about me. I am doing fine," Stacy smiled.

"Okay, Uncle Stacy. How did you find us?" Crystal asked.

"It's always my business to keep ahead of the Commonwealth Authorities and the Navy. One of my agents on Academy tipped me off about your whereabouts on the way to Academy. And my other agent told me about the one who tipped off Rebecca and informed the Navy Security about your port of arrival at the Academy. Also, my agent planted a transmitter on your ship. You need to change whatever your plans are. My guess is you are out for revenge, which is not a good idea. The Navy Security is too big and powerful to bring down."

"You know what happened to us on Lizard Planet," said Tom.

"Yes, and you have every right to get back at Allen for what he did to your family."

"Allen!" said Tom. "He is just a go-between. It's my father, Admiral Melnyk, who is behind it all."

"Not really," said Stacy. "Your father is a self-serving, ambitious Navy officer but not a murderer. Allen is the man you want, not your father."

"But Melnyk murdered my father," said Crystal.

"So we all thought," said Stacy. "I'm not so sure. Not only that, but I believe Mark is still alive."

Crystal was desperately holding back her anger. "How can you be so sure?"

"I can't, but one of these days I hope to find out more than I do now. One of my agents came across a follow-up report on a missing yacht from the cooperative mining corporation. The report was recovered from the ruins of their mining corporation's headquarters because of the Commonwealth's war with the Thracian Empire. The report is heavily damaged, and we don't know where the yacht was missing, but we know this: During their investigation, two ships were found on a planet and both sustained damage. One of the ship's flitters was missing, and the ship is named *Marvel.* The rest of the report is missing. With the flitter missing, it can only mean the crew is alive and has left the area."

"After all these years, my father may be still alive," Crystal whispered as she sat down.

"I'm sorry I couldn't give you more information," said Stacy.

"Uncle Stacy, my mother told me never to give up hope, as hope always finds its way home. You have given me hope about finding Father again," Crystal said as she hugged Stacy.

Stacy took a half step back and said, "I have one thing to ask you. Who is Bert?"

Crystal and Tom looked at each other in surprise.

***

Two Navy personnel, Captain Allen Bergen and Commodore Halley, watched from the control tower as the Thracian ship arrived at the civilian spaceport. The Thracian ship hovered a short distance above the landing spot, then moved to a reserve area and rested. For the longest time, the ship sat silently, immobile.

"What are they waiting for, Allen?" said the Commodore.

The captain turned to the flight controller and asked, "Ask if they need any assistance."

"I have asked already, but there is no response."

"Send a security party for inspection," said the captain.

The Commodore watched as the security rushed to the ship and entered. Moments later, one of the security members exited the ship and arrived at the control tower. "Captain Bergen, this is all we found," as the security agent handed over a paper note.

The captain unfolded the paper, read the note, and sighed. The captain gave the note to the Commodore. The written note said, 'Nuts to You.'

"I don't understand," said the Commodore.

"It means, sir, that we have been taken for a fool again."

"Find them," the Commodore said as he left the control tower.

Allen looked intently at the two men and one woman in civilian clothes, all sitting in their chairs around the cherry table.

"Room Computer, secure the room," Allen ordered.

"Room secured," said the computer as the room was shielded against listening devices and all the doors locked.

The three looked at each other, wondering why there was extra security.

"We have a mole," said Allen. "Both here and at Planet Lizard. They knew every step we took to tender the Steiners. Jake, where are this girl, Katy, and this Thracian?"

"We don't know. We assume that they are with the Stevenson's and may be hidden on Midway or somewhere else."

"Morris, what did you find?"

"For the last five days, all off-world traffic has appeared normal and is scheduled as per registeration."

"Jackie?"

"There is nothing out of the ordinary with the Navy Security or with the Commonwealth authorities. We don't seem to be on their radar, so we should be okay. But I think it's reasonable to assume that the Steiners are both here at the Academy or soon will be. Have you found a replacement for Chloe?" said Jackie.

"Not yet," Allen replied.

"I have one if you need someone reliable," said Jackie.

"I'll keep that in mind. Morrie, keep your people busy. Jake, find this mole. You two may go."

The two men rose from their chairs and left the room. After they had left the room, Allen said,

"After our assignment is complete, I want Jake and his men off-world and eliminated."

"I agree, but I don't think it will solve our problem."

"Why do you say that?" Allen asked.

"I don't think there is a mole but rather an outside agent involved."

Allen knew better than to argue with Jackie and asked, "Do you have any idea who it might be?"

"No, but I am willing to bet that they are savvy and are working with the Steiners."

Allen rose to his feet and walked over to touch a blank wall. A map of the world appeared, and he stared at the screen.

"Where are you, Tom?" Allen whispered.

Jackie stood beside him and said, "I don't think you need to worry so much about Tom. It's Crystal you need to worry about."

Allen replied, "Perhaps you are right. I will see you tomorrow night at the same time."

"Watch your back," said Jackie, as she exited through the door.

Allen stared back at the map and waved his hand as it reformed back into a plain wall.

Allen touched his Comlink and said, "Have my taxi ready, please," to no one in particular.

Allen put on his cap and coat and left his office. When he stepped outside, Allen noticed a taxi had just arrived and stopped in front of him as the rear side door opened for him.

Allen sat down and said, "Computer, take me home."

The taxi rose a foot and began to travel along the freeway when a female head popped up from the front seat.

"Hi, Allen, Are you looking at me?" which was the last thing he remembered.

***

"Mr. Steiner, we are just about finished. Your contact lens matches Allen's iris. The coated, porous silicone skin covering your hand and face is the same as Allen's. We modified your shoes to match his height. Let's dress you up in his clothes. The identity microchip in your cap is identical to Allen's implant. Keeping that cap on your head is critical. I think we are finished. You are good to go."

"Thank you, gentlemen. Please inform your employer that your skills are superb," said Crystal.

"We will. As for Allen, he will be out for another 24 hours. Good luck to you both," he said, as they all left the room.

"How do you feel, Tom?"

"You mean Allen."

"Just testing you," Crystal smiled.

"They did a good job changing your appearance, too," said Tom. "I will meet you back here and later at the Thracian embassy. It's getting late; I better get going now," said Tom.

"Be careful and don't take too long, or I am going to be a nervous wreck," said Crystal.

"Sorry, I can't kiss you."

"There's plenty waiting for when you get back," said Crystal.

Tom shook his head and exited the motel room. It didn't take long for the taxi to arrive at Allen's office at the Navy Security Complex. It hadn't changed much, and it was easy to find Allen's office. Tom allowed the door to scan his eyes and fingerprints. The door slid open, and Tom walked into the room. There were still two hours before the rest of the staff arrived, and Tom quickly went to work. Tom unlocked the desk drawers and safe but found nothing of interest that he already didn't know. Time *to hack into Allen's computer terminal*, he thought.

Tom inserted his app and turned on the machine. *That silly man. No wonder Chloe verbally crucified Allen; he's an addict. Which means, when Allen wakes up, he is going to need a fix*, Tom smiled. *So, who does Allen report to? Commodore Horrent—never heard of him. Wait, what is this, the special operations department? Who's in charge of this department? It's Commodore Halley, Doctor Halley!* Tom thought. *Now, why would Allen have Halley's code to get inside his office?* Tom looked at the time he had left. *It's risky, but I should be able to break into Halley's office.*

Tom shut down the terminal and removed his app. Tom left Allen's office, turned left down the hallway, and took the stairway to the second floor. Across the hallway was Halley's office. The door scanned his fingerprints and iris, and the door slid open. Tom quickly went to work again, slid his app into the terminal, and turned on the machine. Tom hacked his way through the code and downloaded the large files to his implant.

Time is running out, Tom thought as he shut down the terminal and removed his app. Just as Tom stood up, he heard a slump behind the high-backed chair against the corner wall to his left. Tom carefully walked to the chair and turned it around. It was Halley, who was dead with a burnt contact remnant of a stunner at his temple.

Tom backed away and made for the door. The door slid open, and he faced a gun pointed at his forehead.

"I'm sorry," the lady said, but you aren't going anywhere. "Get back inside, Allen."

This woman seems to know Allen. Tom searched through the files he downloaded, as the woman kept talking.

"Where have you been, Allen? You had me looking all night for you."

Tom kept quiet. Otherwise, he would blow his cover. *Jackie. Her name is Jackie. A sniper expert.*

Tom pointed at the dead body, hoping Jackie would keep talking.

"Ya, well, he was becoming embarrassing, and you are to be a fall guy. Only you didn't play the rules of the game."

Tom could hear the early office staff walking along the hallway.

"Ya, I know, but don't you worry, help is on the way," Jackie smiled.

Tom looked out the window and noticed the Navy Security SWAT team had just entered the building. *Are they her rescue team?* Tom thought. *Something is very wrong here.* Tom quickly thought out his plan, lay down on the floor, took out his silver pen, and stunned himself unconscious.

Jackie, puzzled by Tom's action, raised her gun as the door burst in, only to face a hail of gunfire from the SWAT team.

***

"Sir. You should wait for clearance from the paramedics when they come."

"No, I am feeling fine," Tom said as he struggled to get up from the floor.

"You are lucky to be alive."

"Sorry, I am not much of a witness. I must have interrupted Jackie just after she dropped Commodore Halley. If you don't mind, I'd like to get some fresh air."

"Sure, you are free to go. Inspector Jonesborough will catch up with you later today."

"Thanks," said Tom, as he left the building, looked around to see if anyone was looking, and hailed a taxi.

***

"But I thought the cyborg had been eliminated," said Crystal.

"Not according to the files that I downloaded at Halley's office. They thought Bert was one of the cyborgs because of his size and strength. When the Thracian's cyborg detector failed to register, they had Bert scanned and found out he was illegal."

"Bert is an adult, not a fetus. They should have let him go even though he is an illegal genetically modified human being."

"True, so something else is going on in this whole affair. Doctor Halley was going to mind-wipe Bert, but they couldn't find a suitable memory bank for his size and strength. That's why Bert was held in detention until they decided to eliminate him. However, they underestimated Bert's ability to resist several shots from a stunner, and he caught them off guard, as he literally pulverized his assailants and made his escape."

"But why? Bert didn't do anything wrong, other than use a false identity." Then, a thought entered Crystal's mind. "Tom, do you think Doctor Halley was involved in the illegal genetic experiment?"

"That is a real possibility, and if he were involved, he would be charged, convicted and punished by a mind wipe for sure."

"Then why was Halley assassinated and an attempt made on our lives? And where is Bert?"

"I think the answer may be behind you," as they looked down on the unconscious Allen's body.

After Tom removed the sleep collar from Allen, he woke up and sat upright on the bed, naked, and said, "I was never able to find out who sponsored Halley's operation. I am just a small fry."

"I love that word: fry," said Crystal.

Allen took a hint and ignored what Crystal meant. "I don't know why they want you two eliminated; I just follow orders."

"Three," said Crystal in a low, menacing voice. "You forget my daughter, Katy. What is Halley's connection with Admiral Melnyk?"

"They split years ago. Something happened over a disagreement. I am quite sure about that."

"Why?" Crystal asked.

"Melnyk broke Halley's jaw years ago, and they haven't talked ever since. Can I have my clothes back?"

"Not yet," said Tom. "Does Halley operate any genetic lab experiments, other than on the Penitentiary Colony planet?"

"So, you did know about Bert," said Allen. "I was wondering why Halley was so paranoid about you two. Halley is insane, you know."

"So are people who commit murder," muttered Crystal.

Allen shrugged his shoulders and said, "Look, whoever wanted Halley dead wants us dead, too. I can help you both if you help me."

"How?" Crystal demanded.

"Several things. With my contacts, I can get you inside the Cryptologic Department, and I know where Bert is hiding. What I want from you guys are to get me off-world with some credits."

Crystal glared at Allen, then said, "Tom, you handle this," as she walked over to the couch and sat down.

Tom leaned back on his sofa and said, "Under one condition, You are not leaving this motel until after our job is done and we get Bert back. And you get to stay in this motel with the collar around your neck."

Without waiting for agreement, he said, "Now tell me how to get inside."

***

Tom walked around the room and took out his portable scanner to check for any suspicious energy emissions coming from behind the wall or ceiling. Satisfied, Tom sat behind the terminal screen and got to work. Tom inserted his app and checked for the murder investigation earlier today.

Interesting, thought Tom. *Inspector Jonesborough ordered a clampdown on the need-to-know requirement.* Tom opened the profile on Inspector Jonesborough. Tom's eyes opened wide as he saw that he was from the Stevenson home world. *He is certainly qualified for the job, but he is still an outsider for the Navy Security. Who pulled strings to hire him on as a chief inspector? Melnyk, perhaps?*

Nope, another security branch this time. Too risky to break into this one, Tom thought. A drip fell on his cheek, and, surprised, Tom touched his forehead, which was soaked. *Alarm,* he realized. *My subconscious is trying to tell me something, but what? Everything looks normal.* Tom closed his eyes and asked himself, *Okay, what is it?* A thought came to his mind, and he engaged the building security cameras. *SWAT teams! There is no way out. I'm trapped!*

The SWAT team had quickly formed a strategy toward his room. Tom sighed and decided to break all the rules of cryptologic engagement. Tom downloaded the top security files to his implant and forwarded them to another site. Tom got up from his chair and opened the door to face-who else, but Inspector Jonesborough?

***

241

After all her years on Academy, Crystal thought she had a good idea of what to expect in the slums outlining the area near the city. *It's a mixture of hardcore trading and smuggling. It's been a long time since Father showed me how to find my way around in a ghetto trade market. Maintain a straight, hard face, show no interest, and count your luck.* Crystal knew how to find Bert, but where to find him was another question. *Bert has a huge appetite and its near supper time.*

Crystal was hoping to find a center food mall but was dismayed to notice the rundown restaurants, diners, and taverns that were spread throughout the ghetto. *There's no sign of Bert anywhere in this hellhole.* Then, Crystal remembered that Bert loved spaghetti.

Crystal stopped a boy and asked, "Where is the nearest spaghetti factory?"

The lad pointed the way, as Crystal rushed toward that direction. The odour of the Italian spaghetti sauce led Crystal to the restaurants. *It doesn't seem to be a popular spot for some reason*, Crystal thought as she entered through the double doors.

The place was nearly empty. A waiter said, "We are closed today. Come back tomorrow."

Then, a familiar sight at the end of the room brought a smile to her face: *Bert!*

"It's okay, I am with him," said Crystal.

"Hey, guy," the waiter shouted, "Do you know this lady?"

Bert looked up but did not recognize Crystal's disguise. Bert shook his head.

"Out you go, lady."

Crystal burst out, "Bert, don't you ever treat me this way!"

Bert's eyes opened wide because someone knew his name, and he walked up to Crystal. When Bert realized who Crystal was, he laughed and then hugged her.

"Is there somewhere we can talk alone?" said Crystal.

"My table is good as anywhere else. I'm sorry, I can't offer you anything. Our supply is temporarily cut off. How did you find me?"

"It's a long story, Bert, but I want you to know that Commodore Halley and Captain Chloe are dead. Captain Allen is, for now, held in confinement. We need to get you over to the Thracian Ambassador for your protection and wait for Tom to show up and plan our next step."

Bert shook his head, "It will be dark in a few more hours, and my friends will help us sneak out of this ghetto. How is my wife, Tanya, doing?"

"I won't lie to you; she is taking it very hard."

Bert closed his eyes and lowered his head, "So am I."

***

"Why can't I see Tom? He is my husband," said Crystal.

"The nature of the crime involves Commonwealth interstellar security secrets that have been compromised. Therefore, all visitation rights have been suspended. Tom is very lucky he is a Thracian citizen, which nearly created a political fallout between the Thracian and the Commonwealth."

"The Navy Security nearly won the right to a secret court trial and tried to appoint their lawyer for Tom. The Commonwealth had no choice but to hold a hearing. However, it's still behind closed doors. You still can see Tom but only behind the glass wall in the restricted public gallery. It's is the best I can do for you."

"Here is the good part, the Navy Search and Rescue won the right to represent Tom in the hearing. And they say that they protect our own, which has for a very long-time created friction between the Navy Security and the Navy Search and Rescue."

"What if Tom's hearing rules against him?"

"Then the trial will go ahead, and it's likely game over for Tom."

"You have a visitor, Captain Steiner," the guard announced.

"I thought my visitation rights had been curtailed," said Tom. "Who is it?"

"Admiral Melnyk," replied the guard.

Tom looked up in surprise. "Admiral now is it?" as he raised himself from the chair.

Tom looked in the cell mirror to make sure his uniform was in order and walked to the visitor's room. The visitor's room was fitted only for two people and a small table. As Tom sat down, across from Admiral Melnyk, the admiral removed a small device and set it in the middle of the table.

"This device," said the Admiral, "interferes with the cams in this room by playing a computer-generated, pre-recorded conversation. We have five minutes to ourselves before I will end our meeting."

Admiral Melnyk continued, "That was very clever of you to steal those files and discreetly transfer them to my department. What do you want from me to keep it quiet?" the admiral demanded.

"I want names," Tom replied. "Who pulled strings in hiring Halley and Inspector Jonesborough?"

Admiral Melnyk let out a huge breath and, puzzled, studied Tom for a moment and said, "Is that all you want?"

"Yes, sir."

Melnyk smiled, "That's the first time you have shown me respect by calling me 'sir'! Why do you call me sir after what I did to you and your mother?"

"I guess if it weren't for you, I wouldn't be here talking to you, sir. And God has a purpose for everything in life around us all. I still trust God. Things will still work out okay in the end."

"They sometimes do," the admiral muttered. "Get ready to record the name," as Melnyk told Tom the same name of both men.

"Tom, I made a huge mistake ignoring you. I think we would have made a good team together."

"I'm sorry, sir. Too many ambitions corrupt the soul," said Tom. "Besides, with all due respect, your threshold age is ten years from now."

Melnyk stared silently ahead, then slowly shook his head, removed the device and put it back in his pocket.

"On your feet, Captain," said the admiral. When Tom stood up, the admiral held a salute to his head, waiting for Tom to return the acknowledgment.

When the Admiral left the room, Tom quietly whispered, "I would never have expected that in a million years."

***

Crystal sat in the court gallery next to Inspector Jonesborough while Tom sat next to his attorney, Major Paulina Craig, at the front defendant's table before the judges, which consisted of four admirals and four Commonwealth civilian counselors. Among the eight judges, they voted who would be the chairman and they selected a civilian, Judge Lea.

Judge Lea Lam said to the guard, "Seal the door."

Judge Lea Lam looked at each of the seven judges and received an affirmative acknowledgment to proceed.

"The purpose of this hearing is to gather all relevant evidence, and if substantiated, may proceed to a Navy court-martial."

"Captain Steiner," Lea Lam announced. "You are charged with unauthorized use of the Cryptologic Department, the use of a disguise to impersonate a military staff member, known as Captain Allen, assisting an enemy, and misconduct in operations. How do you plead?"

Major Craig stood and said, "My client pleads not guilty, my lady."

"The prosecutor may proceed."

The prosecutor stood up and said, "My lady, I request Inspector Jonesborough to take the stand."

***

Crystal was pleased by the fairness of the hearing. Hours had moved by quickly when Mayor Craig made her final request.

"I request one final witness, Admiral Brean, to take the stand," said Major Craig. When the Admiral was seated, Major Craig took out a device from the case and put it on the table.

"Admiral Brean, do you recognize this device?" said Major Craig.

"My lady," the prosecutor protested, "any devices without pre-approval are banned from this court."

"My lady, I agree," said the defendant. "But this device is only a replica, not the real thing. I assume everyone recognizes the appearance of this Thracian device and its purpose?"

Their discomfort and silence spoke volumes.

"I assume, Major Craig, you have a valid reason for bringing up this forbidden device in the hearing."

"I do, my lady; this device is the sole reason why Captain Steiner was forced to protect himself and his family. Twenty years ago, Captain Steiner, as the chief administrator on a special assignment organized the installation of this device on all spaceport terminals in the Commonwealth's four sectors."

"As you all know, this device has proven to be a valuable asset. Unfortunately, one year ago, another…"

Judge Lam intervened, "Chose your words carefully."

"Yes, my lady. Another person was discovered by accident. Captain Steiner felt that a decision was needed to cover a small gap in the device's installation. When Captain Steiner forwarded his recommendation, he was removed from the special assignment. Three months ago, Captain Steiner was asked to be reassigned as a consultant to the newly appointed administrator for the same special assignment. Shortly after, the Steiner family took their vacation on Lizard Planet."

"Now, let's sum up. From what we know so far, an attempted assassination on Captain Steiner and his family was ordered by someone within the Navy Security. There was an order for Captain Steiner's arrest for what was proven to be a false accusation on arrival as well as a charge of the murder of

Commodore Halley, which of course was committed by Lieutenant Jackie. All with the Navy's signature under the direction of Admiral Brean."

"Are you accusing me?" said the admiral.

"Not at all, Admiral. My apologies, but aren't you ultimately responsible for any misconduct within your department?"

"I am not obliged to answer that question," said the admiral.

"Of course not, Admiral Brean."

"However, someone in your department is responsible for the misconduct."

"I assure you, I will find out who is responsible," said the admiral.

"Oh, I am sure you will find the culprit very soon, Admiral. Perhaps I can help you."

"What do you mean by that?" the admiral asked.

"Whoever is responsible for the misconduct is very likely a close friend of yours."

"I have many friends, and they are all good men and women," the admiral said, noticeably annoyed.

"I agree with Admiral Brean. All good people. But I'm not talking about a Navy member. I'm talking about a civilian. Would you mind informing us of who are some of your closest civilian friends in this room, Admiral?"

"Everyone here knows that Inspector Jonesborough is a good friend."

"Is there anyone else in this room?"

"No," said the admiral.

"And who is a good friend of Inspector Jonesborough in this room?"

"I am not sure... what are you getting at," said the admiral.

"What I'm getting at, is none other than Counselor Stamkos. CATCH," she shouted, as she threw the device.

Counsellor Stamkos caught the device with both hands, and froze, motionless. The entire room was speechless and horrified as they realized Counsellor Stamkos was a cyborg.

Inspector Jonesborough took advantage of the guard's distraction and seized his weapon. Crystal aimed for the inspector's throat with her thumb, and with the other hand, grabbed hold of his wrist that held the gun. The guard retrieved his gun, swung the inspector around, and slammed him against the wall. Crystal unlocked the door as other guards entered the room. The inspector was gasping for air from his injured, bloody throat.

Tom quickly walked up to Crystal and held her in his arms.

"I should be satisfied for what he did to Katy, but I am not," said Crystal. "I wanted to hurt him so bad."

"I know, I know," Tom whispered.

***

"Off-World Flight 1775, now ready for all passengers for destination Midway. Proceed to Lobby 14 A," the PA announced.

"This is where I say goodbye," said Bert.

"Give my regards to Tanya, Uncle Jayson and the rest of the family," said Crystal.

"I heard Katy is doing well in rehab and will soon be on a flight home," said Bert.

"I will be leaving the next day to meet up with Katy and take her home," said Crystal.

"I am glad to hear that. Where is Tom?"

Crystal sighed, "Tom has an appointment with Melnyk. I am not sure what it's all about."

Crystal hugged Bert and said, "Goodbye."

Bert turned and walked through the security gate.

"Admiral Melnyk is ready to see you, Captain Steiner," said the receptionist.

Tom walked past the receptionist and entered the admiral's office. Tom gave the admiral a formal salute and sat down in the chair.

The admiral stared at Tom for several moments, then asked, "Tom, when did you first know the truth about the robots and cyborgs?"

"It was the lost robot in the forest on planet Green Shield that made me suspect that something wasn't right. And things progressed from there."

"Tom, I know you don't trust me and deservedly."

"Why is it so important for you to know?" Tom asked.

"Because the battle isn't over yet and may never be. If it wasn't for you, that cyborg, Stamkos, with Halley's help, would have created more human cyborgs right under our nose. If it weren't for the Thracian device, the cyborg would have shut down his mind and melted."

"We were able to record his memory, and we found out that they have a backup plan, but the cyborgs don't know what the plans consist of. It seems you are always bumping into the cyborgs and messing up their operations. "

"I think you are giving me too much credit when the credit should be given to the unseen hand."

"You believe in your God, like your mother, don't you? Never mind answering that," the admiral sighed. "How did you first encounter the robot that led to the truth about the cyborgs?"

"Twenty-five years ago, when Crystal and I were on Green Shield, the robot I fought against said just before it died, 'Now I go back where I belong.' That was my first clue."

"Do you understand why, for a hundred years, we have kept the secret about the robots and the cyborgs?"

"Not really, but I can guess. You guys are afraid of all the cults. If mad scientists should ever find out there are spirits from Hell, they may enable them to take over the metal or organic bodies. Like back during the robotics era a hundred years ago; when humanity was nearly destroyed."

"Tom, the Thracian and us are the only advanced civilizations we know of that have defeated those essences."

"You left out the Meloson," said Tom.

"Okay, that's three. To this day, we still don't know how those essences took over the bodies. That's why, robots, cyborgs, genetically-modified humans, and advanced androids are banned. We need your help to find the robots and cyborgs' new home base before they get to it first."

"Not now. Perhaps after Katy is grown up and is safe, then we will talk about it and after the downfall."

"What downfall?"

"In my opinion, there will be a civil war between the Commonwealth and the Navy Security in less than ten years.

And no offense, Admiral, but after the downfall, you've only got another few years before the threshold age."

"Perhaps," replied the admiral. "I have one final question: How did you know Counsellor Stamkos was a Cyborg?"

"Most of the cyborgs are clones; Counsellor Stamkos resembled the clone I fought on the ship to Midway."

The admiral was speechless, then nodded his head in admiration of Tom.

"Permission to leave, sir."

"Granted," said the admiral.

***

Nearly 11 years have gone by since Tom's hearing, Crystal thought. *Tom was right about the civil war. It's like his favorite saying 'It is just another time cycle for war and peace. New technology will emerge. Life starts over again from the ashes!' Katy has grown into a beautiful 23-year-old lady and has the smarts of her father. She is safe on Midway. I learned a lot from my father, Mark, but Tom has taught me how to forget the hurtful past. I even found myself quoting some of Tom's verses from his Bible. Imagine that!*

Looking down on this frozen planet is a narrow, 1500-mile-wide temperate warm zone. If my father is still alive, he will be 117 years old. So much time has been wasted. Could Father and I reconcile after I let him down so many years ago? One thing I always remember is my father's saying 'We are the sum of our experiences.' Whatever is down there, I am sure it will be a wonderful surprise.

"Sir," the communication officer announced. "We have found the ship, *Marvel!*"

My heart skipped a beat!